Library Without Walls

Plug In and Go

Compiled by Susan B. Ardis

Library of Congress Cataloging-in-Publication Data

Ardis, Susan.
      Library without walls : plug in and go / Susan Ardis.
        p. cm.
      ISBN 0-87111-422-4
      1. Libraries--United States--Special collections--Data bases.
I. Title.
Z688.D38A73   1994
026'.000973--dc20   93-47261
                                      CIP

Printed on recycled paper.

Contents

Susan B. Ardis
editor

INTRODUCTION

This book got started because a number of us at the University of Texas had questions about the future and we didn't want to be caught by surprise.

- Where are libraries in general going?
- Where in particular is our own library going?
- Is "the library without walls" really possible?
- What do the changes in information delivery and storage actually mean for libraries?

We were all experiencing the impact of technology and wondering whether technology would indeed lead us to an information nirvana. Could we learn more about technology and would this knowledge help us get ready for the future?

One advantage of working in a large academic library is the availability of collegial communications — the chance to kick an idea around, to be "dumb" among friends rather than in public, and to argue and disagree in a friendly fashion. Once we started thinking about the electronic library, we decided that this should really be a local SLA discussion. This book is the result of our discussions, arguments, and meetings. The contributors are from a range of libraries — some are corporate librarians, some academic, some managers, some reference librarians, and one has her own library service company. But all of us share a common interest in self-education and the future of our profession. Because we hope this will be an ongoing discussion, we have included, when possible, the Internet E-mail address of each author, as well as his or her work address. Please feel free to communicate with any of us.

Another advantage of working in and around a large academic library is access to all kinds of information from many perspectives. One very relevant document was the American Information Industry Association's classification of information packages. This list helped us to see information access in an organized way, and it demonstrated clearly what is happening.

- Content Packages: books, journals, newsletters, magazines, newspapers, microfiche, film, video tapes and discs, CD-ROMs, WORMs, etc.
- Content Services: librarians, information brokers, electronic database providers, news services, financial data services, electronic mail services, etc.
- Information Technology: printing and graphics equipment, office equipment, business forms, microforms, terminals, computers, laser discs and optical media
- Communications Channels (physical delivery): post office, telephone, cable, satellite, mobile and cellular services
- Broadcast Channels: TV, radio
- Integrating Technologies: facsimile, digital switches, modems, gateways, packet switches, voice systems

We quickly saw that the future library must meld content packages, services, information technology, communications, and integrating technologies into something that can be used by everyone regardless of experience. This just confirms what many of us already believed: that the library of the future will not be totally electronic, nor will it even be composed primarily of electronic materials; instead it will be an amalgam of books, journals, databases, images, and other as yet unknown technologies. Just as clearly, the place of electronic materials in the library of the future depends on how well (or poorly) they measure up against the historical library mission to preserve and improve access to recorded knowledge. While the depth of this mission has varied by type of library, the function of providing access has remained relatively constant regardless of library type. These new technologies do raise a number of questions that specifically relate to our mission :

- Who will ensure continuing access to the information and knowledge originally generated, stored, and disseminated in electronic form?
- How will information be reformatted as electronic technology changes, and who will do the reformatting?
- Will there be a need to provide access to materials that will never be reformatted?

It is still too early to know the answers, but we do need to think about these questions.

Like it or not, we are all at the cusp of change. Many of us entered the information business when it was just libraries and museums. True, there was some overlap, but generally, libraries specialized in information transmitted through writing and museums specialized in information found in things. Now information can be transmitted in many ways. We cannot escape the electronic library, but why would we want too? This the wave of the future. We all agree with a statement of U.S. Representative George Brown: "What I never dreamed of yesterday, I can't do without today" *(Chronicle of Higher Education,* June 30, 1993. B1). And to that end we are sharing with you what we learned and our hopes for information access nirvana.

We decided to begin our discussions (and this book) with electronic reference, primarily because this is already with us and it has fascinated many of us for quite a while. We also soon rediscovered that technology in the library is circular--one thing leads to another, and all roads lead to training and marketing. Therefore we close the book with training and marketing.

I. ELECTRONIC REFERENCE

We started our investigation with electronic reference because it is the logical offshootof technologies now quite common in libraries--on-line public-access catalogs (OPACS), electronic circulation systems, and on-line database searching. While these technologies have had an impact on libraries, they have basically automated what we were already doing — they are evolutionary rather than revolutionary. However, electronic reference could be truly revolutionary.

When we think about electronic reference it is often in terms of the "electronic library" or the "library without walls." Electronic reference is the underpinning of the electronic library and this seemed like a good place to begin. As we will see, this area relates to many other emerging technologies, such as imaging and SGML, which will change how we provide reference help.

Larayne Dallas
Assistant Head Engineering Library
The General Libraries
The University of Texas at Austin
LLLJD@utxdp.dp.utexas.edu.

1. BUILDING YOUR ELECTRONIC REFERENCE BASE

Here we will use the phrase "electronic reference" to mean reference service assisted by one of the various types of electronically stored or manipulated databases. These databases, most of which have been developed within the past 25 to 30 years, include indexing and abstracting services, data tables, and cataloging records. The information may be stored on compact disc, computer tape, or personal computer. Ideally these tools save time and ease frustration by using computer power to look through lists more quickly than humans, performing searches nearly impossible for a human, and by allowing dial-up access to information that was previously available, if at all, only with the foresight and budget to have purchased a printed product. The ideal of saving time and frustration may not always be achieved, but we know that few who have used these electronic products are willing to go back to those earlier days.

In the not so distant past many smaller libraries were without electronic reference tools. A good number are still without these aids, but the number and variety of available products and new options for access make it increasingly likely that there is something for every library. User interest and skills bode well for a ready acceptance of the products. For those who are just getting started with electronic reference sources and for those who have been working with some of the sources and want to see what else might be available, this chapter aims to give an overview of the topic. The emphasis is on the information needed before making the most technical decisions and on current products and services. The hope is to give appropriate pointers so that a library staff member will know what needs to be considered and investigated when considering an electronic reference product.

Means of Access: Pay-Per-Use versus Buy or Lease

There are several ways of accessing electronic reference products: dialing up directly to the provider; dialing up to a supplier, such as Dialog, which repackages databases; purchasing CD-ROM or floppy disk versions of the databases; having computer tapes loaded locally for searching on your company's mainframe computer; and using databases available on an electronic network. Some providers also offer, for a fee, to run custom searches for customers; *Chemical Abstracts* and *Petroleum Abstracts*, for example, are both made available in this way.

No method of accessing electronic reference sources is free, although some methods may have the advantage of having some costs absorbed in the company's general overhead expenses. In the case of CD-ROM products or computer tapes, vendors expect payment at the time the product is purchased or leased. Other providers charge a connect fee and bill later for the use; typical charges include a fee for minutes of connect time and a separate fee for the number of records accessed. Telecommunications charges — that is, telephone charges — are a usual add-in or add-on to bills. Some providers offer discounts or require surcharges for special categories of users. Access through the electronic network Internet -- discussed more completely in another section of this book -- is an example of when use may appear to be free. If your company has arranged for Internet access for employees and pays the associated bills, the library budget may not feel any impact.

Electronic databases may be available by only one method or in a variety of ways. The ERIC database (an index to education literature), for example, may be purchased on CD-ROM or on tape, and it may also be used through a middleman by dial-up access. A local-interest data source such as a newspaper index may be available only on CD-ROM. Various databases are available free to users on university electronic networks because the products are supported — paid for, mounted, and made available to outsiders within the confines of lease or purchase agreements — by the university or the university library. In many cases, dialing up to the university library's catalog gives access to a variety of other databases. This author cannot, however, recommend spending valuable time searching for free access to commercially available products in the hope of avoiding buying them. Producers have become wise to loopholes and generally close them the next time contracts come up for renewal.

The option of loading computer tapes on the local mainframe computer implies having access to such a computer and having available the expertise to do the work necessary to make the tapes usable. It also brings up the question of how much use is expected to be made of the databases. Owning or leasing tapes implies more than occasional use or that appropriate access to the information can be had only with the tapes. For example, a library's goal of providing customized searches of United States census records would likely require local ownership of the magnetic tapes and someone ready to write the search programs.

Dial-up use of many electronic database products means a direct fee-for-use link. More use means a bigger bill. The advantage is that charges are based on the amount of use; usually, the library does not pay for times when the service is not needed, although some services require a start-up or membership fee. CD-ROM products are paid for whether or not they are used (and are likely to seem expensive) but may be good buys in situations where much use is expected, especially when library users do their own searches. Dial-up services have typically been less user-friendly, requiring more training for use than CD-ROM products and having the pressure of the clock ticking off dollars. CD-ROM products have the disadvantage of requiring multiple discs for a large file. That means searching each disc separately, which is inconvenient compared to searching the entire database at one time as is common with other forms of electronic access.

The Providers

Who provides these electronic reference products? Ultimately, of course, responsibility for a product goes back to the organization that actually sponsors the project and arranges for the data entry, but middlemen play an important role in making available the goods. For example, no matter what electronic or print form *Psychological Abstracts* takes, the American Psychological Association is still responsible for compiling the database from which these products are generated, but various companies contract with the APA to provide dial-up or CD-ROM access to a repackaged version of the database. Dialog is a well-known example of this type of vendor. Dialog provides access to over 400 electronic databases via dial-up (and to some of the same databases on CD-ROM). The search commands and data presentation are uniform across all available Dialog files. Dialog also offers training and user assistance.

Other well-known middlemen include BRS, Lexis/Nexis, Orbit, Westlaw, Silver Platter, and STN. Wilsonline (Wilsondisc in its CD-ROM incarnation), though similar in its role of presenting multiple databases with common search commands, offers only its own indexes, those of the H. W. Wilson Company.

"Bibliographic utility" is the phrase used to describe a special type of database producer. Major examples of the databases of such producers are OCLC and RLIN. The databases contain records for the holdings of libraries that are affiliated with the producer. Sharing cataloging is an important purpose of these cooperative efforts, and easier bibliographic verification facilitates reference service. Indication of library ownership assists interlibrary loan departments (more about this below) and may help individual users find a nearby library that owns a needed item. Full use of the available services requires membership in the bibliographic utility or, in the case of OCLC, membership in the regional organizations that serve a gateway function for the larger organization.

With the increasing popularity of CD-ROM products, it seems that everyone who can get together any kind of electronic product is doing it. Various agencies of the United States government, for example, are releasing CD-ROM products, including statistical databases and maps. What have been paper-only handbooks and indexes -- from private publishers as well as government bodies -- are now also available on CD-ROM. Search commands are likely to be unique to the individual product.

Another example of suppliers with a limited number of products are universities (or university libraries) that make available their library catalogs for dial-up (or Internet) use. If the software was developed locally, search commands will probably be unique and will require learning the specifics of the particular catalog. If the software was purchased from one of the library vendors, such as NOTIS Systems, commands are common to other catalogs sharing the software.

The Services and What They Can Do for You

INDEXING AND ABSTRACTING SERVICES

Early and continuing favorites among electronic reference products are the indexing and abstracting services that are best known for indexing the contents of periodicals (but which often include indexing to conference proceedings and other types of specialized publications, or may focus on one type of material, such as dissertations.) Titles from *Readers' Guide to Periodical Literature* to *Meteorological and Geoastrophysical Abstracts, Psychological Abstracts,* and *Ceramic Abstracts* are available for computer-assisted searching and are likely to be available in more than one version (that is, for example, on CD-ROM and by dial-up to a middleman's computer).

The power and speed of computer-assisted searching of indexing and abstracting services make most users unwilling ever to go back to the paper versions. Keyword searching and the ability to easily combine search concepts are two of the most popular features of such services. Being able to print or download search results is another. Typically, the electronic version of an index will have more access points for searching than will the print version. For example, Dialog's dial-up version of *Engineering Index,* called *COMPENDEX* by the publisher, allows searching by journal name and by language. Also, the print version of this abstracting service did not index individual conference papers until the 1990 volumes, but the electronic version began indexing papers in 1982.

Some indexes in electronic form — for example, *Dissertation Abstracts* and *Georef* — offer coverage back to the beginning of the print publication. Many, however, offer only a partial backfile compared with the print version. CD-ROM versions commonly offer even fewer years of coverage than are available in other electronic versions. When purchasing any version of an indexing or abstracting service, the buyer needs to be alert to how much coverage is being offered and to determine how the electronic product compares with the print version. Both testing the product and reading published reviews -- when available -- can help with judging quality and content.

FULL-TEXT SERVICES

Full-text services — such as various files offered through Lexis/Nexis — provide the actual text of documents. Legal documents, journal and newspaper articles, wire reports, and biographical directory entries are among the types of materials offered in electronic full-text. Users, who so often seem to have needed the information yesterday, benefit by being able to immediately read the information they think is needed, especially when the source publication is not owned by the library or when the print version has not yet come in the mail. Through wire stories or newspaper articles, library staff members may be able to verify the congressional report referred to on a television morning-news report and sought by a library user.

Searching full-text files presents challenges to those used to the controlled or relatively controlled vocabularies of printed indexes. Even electronic versions of the typical indexing or abstracting service usually limit searching to terms in the title, abstract, or assigned subject headings. Full-text files may not have these limits. Often every word in the text is searchable; more so than in other types of databases, limits must be applied by the searcher if limits are needed.

INDEXING WITH TEXT

Indexing with text, a hybrid of the two services described above, offers a computer-assisted index giving reference to the separate CD that has the text of the article (or standard, etc.). The text is not searchable and each page appears in image — as a picture of the normal printed page. UMI, in referring to its ProQuest product, calls this "full-image" as opposed to full-text. Photographs, graphs, and other illustrations are reproduced from the print version.

DIRECTORIES, HANDBOOKS, AND ENCYCLOPEDIAS

While directories, handbooks, and encyclopedias in electronic form could be considered a type of full-text, that term is usually reserved for use in describing journal articles, conference papers, and books. Also, reference "books" are worth noting as a separate entry to emphasize the convenience of being able to search them with computer assistance. This use is a good example of being able to expand access beyond library holdings. The print version is likely to be easier to view and use than the electronic version, but occasional use for a fee can add up to savings over the purchase price of the print source.

One example of this kind of material is *Kirk-Othmer Online,* the computer-based version of *Kirk-Othmer Encyclopedia of Chemical Technology*, a respected multi-volume encyclopedia set for use with chemistry, engineering, and other science and technology topics. In the legal field, an example of an electronically available directory is the *Martindale-Hubbell Law Directory,* again a well-known reference source. In this case the title is one of the best known directories of law firms and lawyers. The *Health Devices Sourcebook* is another example of an electronic directory; it gives medical information as described by the title. *GMELIN*, containing information from the *Gmelin Handbook of Inorganic and Organometallic Chemistry*, and *PLASPEC,* a plastics materials selection database, are handbooks with a special relevance to chemistry and engineering interests.

DATA

Data files present numerical or other categorized data -- that is, the actual numbers -- in machine-readable form--instead of referring to a separate publication that must be located in order to obtain the figures. The *PTS U.S. Time Series* file is an example of a data file already organized into searchable categories by the file producer. Others are available in less organized form, waiting for programming to select out data based on the special requirements of the searcher. United States census records — mentioned above — of the various types (business, agriculture, and population) fit this category.

CATALOGING RECORDS

Among the early, breakthrough, electronically based products for library use were the products aimed at sharing library cataloging information.

Bibliographic utilities such as OCLC have changed the day-to-day work of those entrusted with cataloging library materials and led to visible changes for library users. Cataloging and classification work already done elsewhere is very easily shared, and computer-based local catalogs in many libraries are based on records downloaded from the utilities. In a reference situation the ability to search a utility's database may enable verification of a citation or supply enough additional information so that a local library's holding may be more completely searched. For example, a complete cataloging record may give series information about a title being sought so that the piece may be found in the library's unanalyzed holdings for that series. Searching the databases may also help in compiling bibliographies, as when one is trying to determine all titles by a particular author.

INTERLIBRARY LOAN

A logical extension from the shared databases created by the bibliographic utilities is using the information to assist with interlibrary loan service. OCLC and RLIN, for example, allow searchers both to see which libraries show ownership for a particular title and to use an interlibrary loan subsystem to make a request — via computer —to an owning library. One advantage of the shared information is that smaller owning-libraries can be tapped with a good expectation that a piece can be supplied. Holdings information is not limited — as is typical in book catalogs — to the largest libraries, and those making interlibrary loan requests need not go to larger libraries just because those seem more likely to own an item.

Use of the interlibrary subsystems requires membership in the sponsoring organization. Although membership is not required to tap the portion of the database that tells which library owns what, without membership access to the interlibrary subsystem, standard interlibrary loan paper forms — and the mail — would normally be necessary.

LIBRARY CATALOGS

The bibliographic utilities do a good job of providing certain types of information but have their limitations. Sometimes only an individual library's catalog will provide the needed details. A library's catalog might confirm which of multiple library locations own a book, give detailed information about serial holdings, show that a volume is not checked out, include additional files such as staff directories, provide subject access (or improved subject access), and allow easier searching because of file size or enhanced search keys. Catalogers may wish to check other libraries' local cataloging notes.

ORDERING DOCUMENTS

(Also see the section on Document Delivery.) When interlibrary loan will not work or is inappropriate, and a copy of a needed item must be purchased, an electronic ordering system may be the best route. Dialog's Dialorder service is one example of a program offering materials by electronic order. Various of the offerings available through Dialorder are directly tied to files searchable on Dialog. The Dialorder service Derwent, for example, supports the Dialog Derwent World Patents Index files. Method of payment is as specified by the supplier. Some specify that a credit card number must be given with the order or require prior establishment of a deposit account, while others agree to bill later.

GEOGRAPHIC INFORMATION SYSTEMS

Among the products made possible by computer technology are geographic information systems (GISes). Mapping information and statistical data are available in the same computer database, allowing customized searches combining various features from the two categories of information. For example, with the correct information included in the database, average household income could be mapped against boundaries for voting districts or against elevation. CLIMATEDATA, from Hydrosphere Data Products, Inc., is an example of a commercial GIS product. This one combines National Oceanic and Atmospheric Administration (NOAA) weather data with mapping information and promises analysis in areas including energy consumption.

SPECIALTY PRODUCTS

Almost any sort of text or data file is a candidate for electronic access, so the feeling might be, "This is surely available electronically; all I need to know is where it is." This is not to say that the electronic format is better than other options, but the possibility of dial-up access may get an answer not otherwise quickly available.

Equipment

Not usually the first consideration but still a vital part of using electronic reference services is the equipment to be used. A novice will typically need assistance in selecting or adapting equipment and in initially setting up to use a product. An existing personal computer (in the generic sense) is normally sufficient for getting started with dial-up services, even if it is not a very powerful computer. CD-ROM products typically benefit from — and, to work reasonably well, may require — more powerful computers and do require accessories — most notably, a CD-ROM player to read the CDs and communicate with the computer. A printer needs to be available at some convenient location even if it is not attached to the workstation.

These very general statements are certainly not enough to really get a new person going; the hope is that someone with at least a bit of experience with installing and maintaining personal computers can be found to give assistance. When no one of that description can be found, company representatives, equipment manuals, and installation instructions can sometimes substitute. A general word of advice is that more is better and bigger is better. That translates into securing — within budget restraints — the more powerful computer, the faster modem, and the CD-ROM reader with more slots. A plan to begin use of a certain electronic reference product should not be so modest that the need for equipment is underestimated.

One phrase to know is "communications software." Procomm, Smartcom, ProSearch, PC Talk, and other software programs assist with dial-up access to electronic services. They are used to automatically dial the appropriate phone number to reach a communications network or direct service and then give passwords and other required information to log on successfully. Also they use preset commands to activate printing, to log off, and to perform similar kinds of functions. Advocates can be found for any of the standard programs; when none of them is familiar to the person who will be needing one, it is wise to use the same program that is used by a helpful someone else in the organization or by someone else who can conveniently be called upon when questions arise.

CD-ROM products do not require dial-up software, but when a computer workstation is being used for more than one product or application, a menu interface is a helpful addition. One useful function of the menu interface is to alert users to the various indexes available. They also help users easily tell the computer which software is needed for the application selected or give users options such as "format a disc for downloading."

Pursuing New Routes and Justifying It to the Management

When it comes right down to buying electronic services and deciding which route to take when various options are available, additional information will be needed. A helpful and more in-depth introduction to options in electronic reference is available in Bill Katz's book *Introduction to Reference Work*. To keep up with news and developments, read journals such as *Online* and *Database*. It is the vast area in between that can be the most difficult to pin down — getting the best information to help in deciding which product (in which format) to select and to give you reasons to give the managers in seeking support.

The vendors themselves serve a very useful role as a source of information. Demonstration products, company representatives, and company literature all help in decision making. Bias is expected—that is part of the job of selling — and the careful buyer needs to exert usual caution. Sometimes a product is available only in one electronic version. If that is the product you need, you will probably take what is being offered, but you'll still want to be prepared by having knowledge of what is promised by the producers. Most of us prefer not to have made any statements to library users about the soon-to-be-offered "searching back to 1980," when it turns out to be only "back to 1989."

Contacts at other libraries likely have their own biases but can give another point of view in evaluation. It is great to have a trusted source who is using exactly the product you have in mind, but someone using the same software — say, a Silver Platter CD-ROM product — even when the exact index is different, can still advise about such things as ease of software use, problems with installation, and timeliness of mailings.

Reviews are available in some cases. For example, the "Sources" section of *RQ,* the journal of the Reference and Adult Services Division of the American Library Association, contains database reviews. Articles in *Online* and *Database* may give an overview of what databases and options are available in a certain field or subject area. Finding out about reviews and overview articles and then getting hold of them in a timely fashion may be difficult, however, without access to indexes like *Library Literature* and suitable access to the journals.

Following the advice of Dennis Trombatore in his chapter on marketing, we know that this point — the one at which you are trying to decide what to buy — is properly reached only after an examination of how acquisition of the product will fit in with the marketing plan of the library staff. Will the product help the library serve the organization's mission? Some would note the "gee whiz" value of a new electronic gadget and say that this sort of thing is what helps dispel the image of the library as old-fashioned and not necessarily necessary in the modern era. However, we know that when library staff does reference work for those in other parts of the organization, those others probably don't see firsthand how the work is done, and are not likely to "gee whiz" except when needed services become faster or better or are introduced for the first time.

Still, when special start-up funds are necessary or when a manager is required to give approval for such things as electrical work and computer purchases, for a manager of a certain type, a high-tech demonstration may be just the thing to seal the deal. The library staff will, however, want to have a more solid foundation for long-term success. For managers of all sorts (and for themselves), the library staff will need to be ready with an explanation of what a new product is expected to do and how it will help provide better service.

For example, in a library supplying information to chemical researchers and with a relatively stable budget, staff members may realize that valued chemical reference sets can continue to be afforded in paper copy only by cutting other materials purchases or by taking money from another part of the budget. They realize that an alternative is to subscribe to STN on-line service and use at least some of the reference sets on a pay-per-use basis. Based on observations of researcher use and on knowledge of use by library staff, the staff is able to prepare a comparison of the cost of subscriptions with the estimated cost of dial-up use, and project savings. An added benefit, as far as the library budget is concerned, is that billing to research accounts can now more easily include cost recovery for use of the reference sets.

Summary

The varying needs of individual organizations and their libraries mean that there is no single answer for the question of what electronic reference services are needed (or at least will be very useful) in the library. Even when two libraries are very similar in size and in the type of organization served, decisions made concerning electronic reference are very likely to differ. In other words, as with other types of collection development, there is more than one possible right answer. As noted earlier, however, with the wealth of electronic reference products available, there is likely to be something of interest for every library. Members of the library staff will want to consider what products are available, which can be afforded, where electronic assistance seems most likely to advance productivity, and which of these options can be supported to the organization's management.

SOURCES FOR MORE INFORMATION

Directories and Texts

CD-ROMs in Print. 1987- . Westport, CT: Meckler, 1987- .

Directory of Electronic Journals, Newsletters, and Academic Discussion Lists. July 1991- . Washington, DC: Association of Research Libraries, Office of Scientific and Academic Publishing, 1991- .

Ensor, Pat and Steve Hardin. *CD-ROM Periodical Index: A Guide to Abstracted, Indexed, and Fulltext Periodicals on CD-ROM.* Westport, CT: Meckler, 1992.

Gale Directory of Databases. Jan. 1993- . Detroit: Gale Research, 1993-

In 2 volumes: v. 1, Online databases; and v. 2, CD-ROM, diskette, magnetic tape, handheld, and batch access database products.

Katz, William A. *Introduction to Reference Work*, 6th ed. New York: McGraw-Hill, 1992. v. 1, Basic information sources; and v. 2, Reference services and reference processes. Particularly see "Computers and Reference Service" (v. 1, part I, no. 2), but look in both volumes for more information on the topic.

Kessler, Jack. *Directory to Fulltext Online Resources 1992.* Wesport, CT: Meckler, 1992.

Periodicals

Database. 1978-. Online, Inc., 462 Danbury Road, Wilton, CT 06897-2126; 203-761-1466.

Online. 1977-. Online, Inc., 462 Danbury Road, Wilton, CT 06897-2126; 203-761-1466.

RQ. 1960-. American Library Association, 50 East Huron St., Chicago, IL   60611-2795; 800-545-2433.

Bibliographic Utilities

OCLC Online Computer Library Center, Inc., 6565 Frantz Road, Dublin, OH   43017-0702; 800-848-5878 and 614-764-6000.

RLIN. The Research Libraries Group, Inc., 1200 Villa St., Mountain View, CA   94041-1100; 415-962-9951.

Utlas International Canada, 3300 Bloor St. West, 16th Floor, West Tower, Etobicoke, ON   M8X2X2, Canada; 800-268-9892 or 416-923-0890.

WLN, 4224 6th Ave., S.E., P.O. Box 3888, Lacey, WA   98503-0888; 800-DIALWLN (800-342-5956).

Other Providers of Electronic Reference Products

BRS Online and BRS Software Products, 8000 Westpark Drive, McLean, VA   22102; 800-289-4277, 800-955-0906, and 703-442-0900.

Data-Star, North American Office, D-S Marketing, Inc., Suite 110, 485 Devon Park Drive, Wayne, PA   19087; 215-687-6777.

Dialog Information Services, Inc., 3460 Hillview Ave., P.O. Box 10010, Palo Alto, CA   94304-0993; 800-3-DIALOG (800-334-2564) and 415-858-3785.

Hydrosphere Data Products, Inc., 1002 Walnut, Suite 200, Boulder, CO 80302; 800-949-4937 and 303-443-7839.

Information Access Company (IAC), 362 Lakeside Drive, Foster City, CA   94404; 800-227-8431 and 415-378-5000.

Lexis/Nexis; Mead Data Central, Inc., 9443 Springboro Pike, P.O. Box 933, Dayton, OH   45401; 800-227-4908 and 513-865-6800.

ORBIT Online, 8000 Westpark Drive, McLean, VA   22102; 800-456-7248 and 703-442-0900.

Predicasts, Inc., 11001 Cedar Ave., Cleveland, OH   44106; 800-321-6388 and 216-795-3000.

Questel; North American Office, Questel, Inc., 2300 Clarendon Blvd., Suite 1111, Arlington, VA   22201-3367; 800-424-9600 and 703-527-7501.

SilverPlatter Information, Inc., 100 River Ridge Road, Norwood MA 02062-5026; 800-343-0064 and 617-769-2599.

STN International, c/o Chemical Abstracts Service, 2540 Olentangy River Road, P.O. Box 3012, Columbus, OH   43210-0012; 800-753-4CAS (800-753-4227) and 614-447-3600.

Westlaw; West Publishing Company, 610 Opperman Drive, Eagan, MN 55123; 800-328-0109 and 619-687-7000.

II. OBTAINING THE INFORMATION

Once you have found out what is available, the next step is to get it. Someday, when we are in information nirvana, all we'll have to do is click and there it will be--right on our workstations or TVs. Until this happens, we will need to use a variety of techniques. The next two articles deal with a very important topic--getting copies of the information you have discovered. The first, by David Flaxbart, is really an overview of document delivery, including interlibrary loan and commercial services. It offers some important points about dealing with net lenders--large archival collections. The second, by Renee Daulong, is from a little different point of view--that of the commercial vendor. We can all learn and benefit from hearing from a vendor who knows us and our needs intimately. Both articles provide insight and "a view from the trenches."

Interlibrary loan will not go away because many individuals are unwilling to buy magazines and books or pay for article copies. Some interlibrary loan users may not be aware that materials are generally borrowed from tax-supported institutions and that most of these are under pressure to reduce expenditures. No doubt about it, interlibrary loan is heavily subsidized by taxpayers. We all need to be aware that unless an article is purchased directly from the producer (IEEE, for example), tax dollars are probably involved somewhere.

David Flaxbart
Chemistry Librarian
The General Libraries
The University of Texas at Austin
LLDF@utxdp.dp.utexas.edu

2. DOCUMENT DELIVERY: INTERLIBRARY LOAN, AND BEYOND

Even though your library may not have much in the way of an on-site collection, a good part of your demand will be for paper documents in the traditional sense: books, journal articles, patents, conference papers. You will be faced with obtaining these items for your patrons "just in time," whereas larger libraries collect and house them "just in case." Identifying a requested document is one thing, and getting hold of it is another; but getting hold of it *quickly* will be the crucial measurement of your library's effectiveness in meeting the demands of your clientele-- and ultimately justifying your library's existence.

People tend not to plan ahead, so when a patron's need for information arises it's likely to be urgent. The computer has increased the library's ability to deal with this immeasurably, but it has also widened the accessibility of global information, increasing the likelihood that patrons will stumble across obscure but urgently needed references.

While the growing availability of documents in full-text electronic format promises to grow in the future, remember that only a tiny fraction of "published" information is currently available that way and what is available usually lacks the graphics, illustrations, and special characters that are crucial in technical literature. Researchers often will accept no substitute for a good paper copy of the original — sometimes a fax copy isn't even good enough.

Steps in the Process

1. Bibliographic verification. Before you order something, you have to know what it is you're ordering and whether or not it exists. You'll quickly realize that literature references supplied in bibliographies, by colleagues, or other informal sources can be so garbled, incomplete, and filled with errors that extensive work must be done just to determine what the item actually is. Indexes and on-line databases make this work much easier, but there will always be a number of requests that simply cannot be verified. Detective work with directories and a telephone will resolve some of them, if you have the time, but after a certain point you have to give up and return the request, asking for more information.

2. *Identifying a supplier.* This is a big step, and we'll go into it in more detail below.

3. *Request submission.* Identifying a source for your document is also a big step. But once you do, choosing a method of submitting the request can have a major effect on your chances of success and your turnaround time. Being able to phone in a request or send it over a computer network can cut down the turnaround time significantly (and likely increase the cost).

4. *Request processing and file maintenence.* While you're waiting for responses, you should have a workable file or database of pending requests. This is something that can be readily automated on a local PC or network, but however you do it you must be able to keep track of what has been requested and what is in process. That way you can report on the status of a request quickly if the patron asks how it's going.

5. *Invoicing and payment.* The accounting associated with using a myriad of external document suppliers can be a headache, but it's equally important in maintaining a quality operation. Deposit accounts with commercial suppliers can help you out considerably, but many services invoice with the item. Again, this is a task that can readily be automated with a number of software packages.

Choosing a Supplier

There are a number of criteria you must weigh before choosing a supplier.

1. *Holdings.* There's no point in submitting a request if the targeted supplier doesn't own the document. Verifying who has what is a soft science at best. Commercial index producers and vendors publish title lists with date ranges that are usually pretty reliable, and patent suppliers are also relatively straightforward. Library holdings are another matter. (This will be discussed below in the context of interlibrary loan.)

2. *Turnaround time.* Speed is very often of the essence. Choose a supplier that you know moves fast--some do, and some don't but say they do. Commercial suppliers and libraries alike often have delivery options other than the mail, but these usually cost more. A "rush" request costs more too, but may not make a significant difference, especially if all your

requests are marked "rush." But the bulk of turnaround time is taken up by processing on the supplier's end, and this depends on how much traffic it has and the size and skill of its staff--things you cannot control, or even guess at sometimes. Again, experience will be your guide for the most part.

3. *Cost.* Document delivery is an expensive operation for a supplier: collection, staff, equipment, and administrative costs make overhead high. For-profit suppliers also need a respectable profit margin to justify offering the service. Most paid services charge upwards of $10 per item for a normal request; a rush job involving special delivery (by fax, express mail, or courier, for example) will of course cost more. Copyright fees and other incidentals are tacked on, and the total can add up fast.

If the information you're obtaining is worth something to your clientele, then its cost can be counted as part of the cost of doing business. Information is not free, and neither is the infrastructure that collects and disseminates it. Remember that obtaining documents on demand is more cost-effective for smaller libraries than subscribing to all the needed journals and services could ever be. Most special libraries do subscribe to their "core" materials, things that are needed on-site so often that document delivery is no longer a cost-effective option. Where you draw the line between access and ownership depends on your clientele, your space, and your budget.

The Options

When you're faced with the task of getting a copy of a paper or report, or the loan of a book, several routes are possible. Again, the format of the material needed will largely dictate which option you choose, as will the desired turnaround time. This section deals only with sources for hard-copy materials; getting information delivered electronically (such as full-text on-line journals) is covered in another chapter.

The hard-copy options are:

1. Interlibrary loan
2. Commercial document delivery
3. Information brokers
4. Author reprints
5. Informal contacts and networks

1.   Interlibrary Loan

Interlibrary loan has long been the "pack mule" of information transfer among libraries. The idea of one library allowing another to borrow its materials, or providing photocopies of its materials, is not a new one, although the technology by which this is accomplished has developed rapidly over the last twenty years. Verification of holdings — figuring out with some sense of accuracy who has what — is much easier since the advent in the 1970s of giant cataloging utilities such as OCLC and RLIN. These shared cataloging databases are intended for and used primarily by academic and public libraries, and the costs for their services and equipment can be prohibitive for smaller special libraries that do not earn credit by contributing their own cataloging. Nevertheless, access to the large union catalogs and holdings lists is very valuable for verification and holdings information, particularly for books and conference proceedings. (A "union catalog" is a generic term for any sort of listing of bibliographic holdings across multiple libraries.)

OCLC is by far the largest such utility, and its statistics are staggering: by mid-1993 over 16,700 libraries around the world were participating in its activities, and they share a database of over *28 million* records for books, serials, AV materials, manuscripts, and data files, for which there are more than *477 million* location listings. Your library doesn't have to be a major cataloging contributor to get access to these resources. OCLC's recent excursions into reference services include EPIC, a search system similar to Dialog's that accesses the main Online Union Catalog and a growing number of other databases as well. Like Dialog, EPIC charges by connect time and records displayed, so you pay only for what you use. FirstSearch is an easier-to-use menu-driven version of the same thing, and it is intended primarily for the end user, not library staff.

Member libraries can also take advantage of bibliographic utilities' interlibrary loan subsystems, which facilitate rapid transmission of requests to potential suppliers. OCLC's ILL subsystem, operating since 1979, routes millions of requests every year among the utility's members (over 45 million total requests by mid-1993) and also supports statistics-keeping and batch-processing software to help with a volume business. If your library does enough document access — particularly for older journals or books — the hardware, membership fees, and telecommunications costs associated with using OCLC's system can well be more cost-effective than using commercial for-profit suppliers, and it is certainly more efficient than mailing typed request forms.

Without access to a utility like OCLC or RLIN, verifying which libraries own what can be a time-consuming and hit-or-miss task. The Library of Congress's *National Union Catalog, New Serials Titles,* and

Newspapers in Microform are massive printed union lists of books and journals and are normally found only in larger libraries. The *Union List of Serials* (3d ed., H.W. Wilson, 1965) remains useful for older journals and obscure foreign titles and is only five volumes long. Chemical Abstracts Service's *CASSI* (Chemical Abstracts Service Source Index) is issued every five years and is extremely useful as a verification source for some 12,000 chemistry-related journals and conferences. It is broad enough to encompass many titles in biosciences, engineering, and physics, but the reliability of its library holdings listings is open to question. Other printed union lists and book catalogs are good for identifying and locating old and ephemeral library material, but they really are no substitute for an OCLC or RLIN record. Nor do they begin to touch the vast grey literature that technical fields have spawned.

In recent years, many libraries have made their on-line public-access catalogs (OPACs) available free of charge to anyone via dial-up modem or the Internet. Searching through these can be laborious, but this may be the only electronic option available to special libraries without OCLC or RLIN accounts. With a handful of good libraries in mind, you can save a lot of time and guesswork by dialing into their catalogs.

The Internet, an international network of networks, is a faster and cheaper avenue to databases and mainframes all over the world. While access to it is generally restricted to educational and governmental institutions doing federal research, there are many ways for commercial enterprises to take advantage of its speed and breadth. Hundreds of library catalogs are now accessible via the Internet, and more come on-line every day. The "telnet" command of the Internet Protocol (IP) is the mechanism for making a real-time connection to a remote computer and tapping its resources. (See Internet chapter.)

A good way to save time with remote access to multiple remote sources is to use your communications software package to set up aliases or macros to connect quickly and automatically, perhaps from a menu system on your workstation. If you're using the Internet, you may want to give your patrons access to these resources on public terminals as well.

Once you have located a holding library, the next task is to submit the request. Libraries have a bewildering array of policies defining whom they'll lend to or copy for, whom they charge, and what they'll lend and what they won't. Some broad generalizations are obvious: libraries rarely lend periodical volumes or issues, reference books, rare or fragile items, or dissertations. But the fine points vary widely. Directories of ILL policies have been published to help borrowing libraries with all these rules.*

* (Needless to say, these go out of date very quickly, but a recent one is Interlibrary Loan Policies Directory, 4th ed., by Leslie R. Morris and Sandar C. Morris. New York: Neal-Schuman, 1991 ISBN 1-55570-090-X.)

Lending libraries will accept requests in a variety of formats: electronically, via OCLC, by fax, and by mail (using the standard ALA request form). Rarely will you be able to request something over the phone, however. On the request you will specify the material needed (a complete and accurate citation is very important), the shipping address, your cost limitations, and other special notes about your needs, including a required notation of copyright compliance and an indication of how you identified the lending library.

Delivery of materials is most often by U.S. mail unless you request otherwise. Obviously, that's the slowest and cheapest method, but if you want something fast there are other options. Fax is now commonly used by most ILL departments and is the preferred medium for rush requests. Scanning/transmission systems like Ariel (a project initiated by the Research Libraries Group, creators of RLIN) also take advantage of optical technology to transmit documents rapidly. Loans of books most often use the U.S. 4th Class Library Rate, but may also be sent by any express mail courier service if you're willing to pay the extra price.

Resource sharing via ILL is rarely free anymore. It's a costly enterprise for everyone involved, and libraries usually pass on charges to the requesting library, which may in turn pass them on to the patron. Special libraries usually pay the charges as part of their cost of doing business. Alternatively, some special libraries might want to use an internal accounting system to charge users or their departments for the services provided.

There are many hidden costs involved in any sizeable ILL operation: staff time, postage, equipment, telecommunications, and photocopying are all part of the overhead involved in providing documents. To recoup these costs, most academic libraries routinely charge special libraries, particularly those within for-profit organizations, fees for book loans and/ or photocopies. The amount can vary widely, but will seldom be less than $5 per article or loan and probably in the $10 to $15 range, depending on the size of the request. Delivery by fax or courier costs extra, as does any rush processing.

Many libraries within a given region or consortium make formal agreements among themselves for reciprocal borrowing and copying. This allows faster, more efficient resource sharing among similar libraries and avoids excess accounting costs. Smaller special libraries, especially those in corporations, may have no significant collections with which to reciprocate and do not contribute to the shared databases larger libraries use. For this reason the technical information center will rarely be eligible to participate in the larger agreements. That doesn't mean you shouldn't make the offer or jump at the chance to join such an agreement, particularly one with similar libraries. It's always better to be part of a group, and making these arrangements for cooperative information transfer is an excellent way to promote your library and expand your options, as well as save money.

The longstanding complaint about ILL service has always been its speed, or more to the point, its lack of speed. Two to four weeks turnaround time is not unusual for a typical U.S. mail transaction even if the request is submitted electronically. Most of this is mailing time and is beyond anyone's control, but processing time on the lender's end also contributes to slow turnaround. You have to consider that most large academic ILL departments handle many thousands of requests a year and that substantial staff time is required to identify material, page it, copy it, package it, bill for it, and ship it out. Many libraries have greatly improved their performance over the years, and some can handle requests very quickly and efficiently. Experience will quickly tell you which libraries are good at it and which you should avoid. Keep a written list or spreadsheet for your staff to consult.

Many studies have looked at ILL turnaround time, and their conclusions tend to agree that regular ILL is faster and more efficient than most people give it credit for. But it is still far from ideal — in some ways new technologies have been loaded onto it without much rethinking of the overall design. After all, a Model T with a Ferrari engine is still a Model T. Expect more changes and improvements down the road as electronic technologies develop, but be aware that the sheer inertia in large library organizations tends to slow change to a snail's pace. In addition, people's insistance on publishing and getting information in hard copy sets inherent limits on transmission that technology can never eliminate entirely.

Even though the bulk of turnaround time is at the supplier's end, you can expedite the transaction by automating as much of your processing as possible. On-line bibliographic and holdings verification using a utility like OCLC, electronic request submission--preferably on the same utility, and automated tracking of your outstanding requests and invoices all will cut down the amount of work you have to do to locate and receive documents. If you choose to use "conventional" interlibrary loan heavily, a full membership in OCLC is certainly worth considering. The hefty fees and equipment and telecommunication costs will be offset by added efficiency in your operation. OCLC's support software will automate most of your ILL functions for you. Do your cost-benefit analysis to see how it might work in your library.

A final point to remember about ILL: don't overdo it. There is a definite etiquette associated with using another library's services. A rule of thumb you should observe is to request from the smallest known supplier that is closest to you. Don't send all your requests to a giant research library in the next state if your local college library owns the title. Other "don'ts":

- Don't send large numbers of requests at once to a single library--you'll get yourself on a blacklist very quickly. Scatter them around. Trying out a number of different suppliers adds to your store of experience, too, and gives you more options for the future.
- Don't make unreasonable requests for speed or size. (Asking for a free copy of a 100-page article isn't likely to win you any friends.)
- Don't send "blind" or unverified requests. If you're not sure if a library owns something, say so on the request form and tell them what you've done already to find out. It isn't good to appear lazy in your suppliers' eyes.

Some "do's":

- Verify your citations in advance, and if you can't, say so on your request form. Large libraries are normally glad to help you figure something out, but don't take that service for granted--do your homework first. Remember that verification has two steps: ascertaining that a particular document actually exists, and determining who is likely to have it.
- Observe the copyright laws. They're complicated and restrictive, but your organization will be open for a great deal of trouble if you're caught violating them. (see the box at the end of this chapter.)
- Finally, *always* reciprocate if the need arises.

If you live by these rules, you'll maintain good relations with your suppliers and benefit from their holdings and their skills.

2.   COMMERCIAL DOCUMENT DELIVERY

Commercial document suppliers may or may not be the fastest and most reliable method to get information — opinions differ — but they are certainly the most expensive. Some libraries use them regularly to the exclusion of other suppliers, while others use them only as a last resort. It all depends on your needs and budget.

Commercial suppliers come in all shapes and sizes. Some are profit-making companies, others are not-for-profit arms of various institutions, and many are directly associated with index producers, publishers, and on-line vendors. Scope, holdings, and prices also vary widely, so it pays to know which suppliers do the best work for the best price.

Document delivery is becoming more closely linked with on-line searching. Major on-line vendors like Dialog and STN have set up document-ordering mechanisms within their networks: if you have a set of search results from a database, you can initiate an order function and request hard-copy of those articles while you're still on-line, sort of like one-stop shopping. The order is automatically routed to a vendor of your choice, and you are billed for the items separately. It can be quite expensive to get documents this way, but it does cut down the time involved in processing at your end; there's no need to verify holders or submit multiple ILL requests. Dialog's service is called Dialorder, and it links you up to document suppliers (though your choices will be largely determined by what database you're searching). STN accesses over 25 suppliers, including a number in Europe and Japan, which you can choose from with the ORDER command. Other on-line vendors offer similar services, but since most literature searching needs can be met by Dialog and STN, they are not discussed here. Check in their database catalogs or on-line help files for further information, or call their customer service numbers.

Remember that even if you're ordering on-line, prices and turnaround times vary.

Choose a vendor according to the needs of the moment. The criteria to examine include:

- format of material needed (journal article? patent? standard?)
- subject matter (chemistry? computers? aerospace? business intelligence? biomedical?)
- turnaround time needed (suppliers vary)
- cost

Ordering a document from a vendor usually means getting a photocopy of the original. The format of the original can determine your choice right away.

Published journal articles, book chapters, conference papers

Most vendors deal in these, within their subject areas. Major on-line vendors like Dialog, Carl Uncover, and Orbit; index producers like ISI (the Genuine Article), EI Information Inc., Chemical Abstracts Service; and many other specialized sources supply plentiful varieties of such materials. (See the list of Major Document Suppliers at the end of this chapter.)

Patents

The U.S. Patent and Trademark Office (USPTO) supplies cheap copies of U.S. ($3.00) and foreign patents, but the service is rather slow. Index producers often supply copies of patents they index--CAS is the best example, a very good source for Japanese, German, and European chemical patents. Commercial patent vendors like Derwent probably have the widest array of services for this format. Other patent suppliers include Air Mail Patent (about $6.00--302-424-7692), Rapid Patent (about $18.00--1-800 336-5010), and British Lending Library (European patents).

Standards

Currency and speed in obtaining standards are often vital factors in the engineering, technical, and legal fields, yet information about standards themselves is often sketchy and hard to find. U.S. industry standards, military specifications (Milspecs), federal regulations and/or laws, foreign national standards, and international (ISO) standards are all part of the array of standards literature you may have to identify and obtain. The matter is complicated by the transient nature of standards: they are constantly being updated and revised, and getting the most current version is very important. No library can hope to maintain a current collection of all of them, so this is an area where commercial suppliers are a particularly useful source. Information Handling Services, Inc. (IHS), Derwent, and Global Engineering are the best known. IHS also leases collections, in microform and CD-ROM formats, of standards, Milspecs, and vendor catalogs that can be very useful in a technical library.*

---

* Because of lease agreements libraries with standards from IHS cannot supply copies of them through ILL. When you order from Global, Global pays royalties to the standards producers. Standards may be copied on-site in libraries open to the public with IHS collections. Note: the authors and editor know of no library that subscribes to a complete set of ISOs--it's just too expensive. The average ISO from Global is about $125.

Technical reports

These also come in all shapes and sizes. NTIS, NASA, EPA, and DOE are major examples of the numerous U.S. government agencies that issue reports documenting research conducted under government contracts. NTIS (National Technical Information Service) is a large federal clearinghouse for most of these and sells paper or microfiche copies of reports on demand. Its indexing service produces *Government Reports, Announcements and Index* (GRA&I) which is available on-line as the NTIS database on Dialog, STN, and other vendors. Large agencies such as NASA and DOE also run their own document delivery and subscription services. Many libraries do not catalog NTIS reports, and as a result these are generally not available through ILL.

Many professional societies also issue technical report series, including AIAA, SAE, SPE, ASME, and many others. The societies usually will sell copies of their reports on demand. Since academic libraries purchase these in annual microfiche sets, paper copies are often more expensive than ordering the report directly from the issuing society. For example, a library purchasing AIAA papers on microfiche will receive a year's worth of paper at one time, so to get a copy of a paper from the current year, it is often best to purchase it directly from the society.

State and local governments, corporations, and universities also can issue reports as part of ongoing or contracted research, but there is little regularity or predictability in them. State or municipal libraries (not public libraries) are the best source for governmental reports, while libraries associated with particular universities (such as MIT, Stanford, Michigan) are the best bet for university reports . Remember that many of these reports are rather obscure and may never have been deposited into the institution's library; they may be available only from the academic department concerned or from the author(s). Corporate reports are usually proprietary information, and these are generally unavailable for dissemination or copying.

Ephemera

In other words, none of the above. Ephemera can include foreign government documents, preprints, unpublished conference papers, in-house or proprietary reports, company newsletters, electronic documents, and just about anything else that doesn't fit into the most common molds. Your options for obtaining these are limited indeed, but index producers (if the item has been indexed, there's always a chance), home libraries, national libraries or depositories, and the authors themselves are your best sources. Commercial vendors tend not to cover ephemeral materials well.

Learning to spot the grey literature--reading between the lines of a citation, in other words--is half the battle. After that, your experience, creativity, and persistence will determine your success in locating these challenging materials.

The field of commercial document delivery and information transfer is growing rapidly as the world's information matrix becomes more complex. Many suppliers are recent additions to the marketplace and are constantly expanding their scope and services. Index producers and on-line vendors, even not-for-profit ones like OCLC and CARL, are becoming more generalized information suppliers, and this trend is likely to continue.

In recent years some major academic libraries have also entered this market, setting up fee-based document delivery services side by side with their older, conventional interlibrary loan departments. These services take advantage of the libraries' large and rich collections and make them available to commercial or private customers for a fee competitive with that of for-profit suppliers. Special libraries not eligible to use regular ILL services can use these newer fee-based services instead. The range and scope of materials obtained from research libraries is much broader than that of commercial suppliers and index producers. Older materials, government information, and ephemera are more likely to be found in such an institution, and the service you receive can be very good indeed. Furthermore, the money spent on this service goes back into developing that library's collections and services, instead of into corporate pockets. The Michigan Information Transfer Service (MITS) at the University of Michigan and R.I.C.E. at Rice University are just two examples; more are being set up every year.

3.   Information Brokers

As long as there is a demand for information, entrepreneurs will always spring forward to supply it. For a fee or by a contract arrangement, these "middlemen" will seek out and obtain desired information or materials for their clients. Primarily they choose to take advantage of local library resources, sending their staff in to locate and copy requested items or borrow books. This saves time for clients unable or unwilling to do so themselves. Some brokers will also go to commercial vendors if local resources prove insufficient and may conduct more in-depth research on demand. Others have expanded into providing in-house services: anything from photocopying to data entry to desk staffing may be contracted out to these library service firms.   In current parlance this is called "outsourcing."

Organizations with libraries on site may not need the services of information brokers, but it's important to remember they're there. If you are working in a library-rich part of the country, such as the Boston-Washington DC corridor, Chicago, or the San Francisco Bay area, brokers may be able to supply information more quickly than conventional libraries or commercial suppliers. It may also be more cost-effective for your organization to contract document retrieval out to brokers rather than using your own staff as runners or obtaining materials from commercial, remote sources. (See the next chapter for more information on outsourcing.)

4.   AUTHOR REPRINTS

Authors frequently purchase from their publishers reprints of articles accepted for publication, and book authors usually receive some free copies of their books. If a document proves impossible to get through conventional channels, and if the author can be located, he or she may have a reprint or copy to lend you at no cost. The author may even be flattered that someone has gone to the trouble to seek him out in a quest for an obscure document. This is occasionally your only option when faced with obtaining an unpublished conference paper. An abstract or summary may have been printed in the conference guide, but the full text may have been distributed only in photocopy form at the meeting itself. That doesn't prevent it from being cited later on, however, and you may be asked to locate it. An author may be your last resort.

5.   INFORMAL NETWORKING

Never underestimate the value of knowing people in the right places. In the course of regular business you will be trading information, documents, and general knowledge with your counterparts across town and around the world. You will get to know researchers, on-line representatives, and librarians. Take advantage of these connections, but never abuse them. Networking with libraries and information centers similar to yours can reap considerable benefits for all involved. You may set up informal copying, document sharing, acquisitions, and reference agreements within your circle, and these can prove very valuable in a pinch. If you happen to be running a one-person operation, these contacts are your link to the outside world and thus are doubly important.

So be sure to attend meetings, get-togethers, training sessions, and other events where this networking takes place. There are no walls or boundaries in the information world, so it will be to your advantage to broaden your horizons and avoid becoming isolated.

The Future

Many people would like to think that the relatively slow copying and exchanging of information on paper is on the way out, to be completely replaced by the fabled "paperless society." In this vision, scanned images and text, digitized for rapid searching and transmission, will make old-fashioned things like books, photocopying machines, and the U.S. mail obsolete. Information providers will be able to locate, request, and deliver documents without leaving their terminals, all at the speed of light.

While this is a pleasing scenario, don't look for it to happen anytime soon. Parts of the necessary technology are in place and improving daily, but we're a very long way from a totally digitized and networked world. The expense of this change, the problems of copyright, and the sheer difficulty of transforming a traditional way of doing things have yet to be addressed.

A Word About Copyright

Copyright laws are like your income taxes: nobody understands them very clearly, but ignoring them will almost certainly get you into trouble. Every operation involved in obtaining or disseminating information runs up against the copyright question sooner or later. Libraries, long dedicated to the free exchange of information and ideas, tend to be handicapped the most by restrictions on the duplication of intellectual property. The doctrine of "fair use" is at the center of this question, and this is an extremely complicated notion.

Basically, it is the responsibility of the *person who copies* a document to ensure that proper credit and/or payment is made to the copyright holder for use of a particular piece of information. Determining who that holder is, and how to pay, is easier said than done, however. If your library is primarily a consumer of documents, rather than a provider, the situation will be more straightforward. You might find you cannot obtain a copy of something from a supplier because of copyright restrictions, or you may have to make periodic payments to publishers or the Copyright Clearance Center for use of documents.

You can get into real trouble if part of your job is to make multiple copies of a document for distribution within your organization. Publishers have successfully sued companies for violating fair-use doctrines and infringing on copyrights. Liability for violations of copyright rests with the organization, and the bigger your parent institution is, the greater the potential damage from carelessness in this area.

Whole books have been written on the intricacies of copyright law, and this is not the place to try to summarize it. You are best advised to examine some basic guides to the subject--written in English, not legalese. Two possibilities are:

Strong, William S. *The Copyright Book: A Practical Guide*, 4th ed. Cambridge MA: MIT Press, 1993. ISBN 0262193302

Dukelow, Ruth H. *Library Copyright Guide* (Copyright information bulletin, 8). Washington DC: Copyright Information Services, 1992. ISBN 0892400676

Nothing is constant where laws are concerned, so remember to look for the most recent materials available.

Some Major Document Suppliers

Listed alphabetically, with location, on-line vendor link (STN or Dialog), associated databases and indexes, and general subject area. Consult documentation for further information.

AIAA Library. (American Institute of Aeronautics and
Astronautics) NYC   Dialog
> Aerospace Database; International Aerospace Abstracts, STAR
> AIAA, NASA, ESA reports, periodical literature
> aerospace engineering and technology

American Geological Institute. GeoRef DDS. Alexandria, VA   STN
> GeoRef; Bibliography & Index of Geology.
> geosciences

Ask*IEEE. Institute of Electrical and Electronics Engineers,
Burlingame, CA   Dialog
> IEEE publications.
> electrical and computer engineering

ASM International, Photocopy Service. Materials Park, OH   Dialog, STN
> Metadex; Metals Abstracts.
> metallurgy

British Library Document Supply Centre. London   Dialog, STN
> all subjects; books, periodicals, ephemera.

Chemical Abstracts Service DDS. Columbus, OH   Dialog, STN
> Chemical Abstracts.
> chemistry, biochemistry, chemical engineering

CAB (Commonwealth Agricultural Bureaux). UK   Dialog
> CABA, CAB Abstracts.
> agriculture, nutrition, forestry, etc.

Derwent Publications Ltd., UK   STN
> World Patents Index.
> patents

Engineering Information Inc., NYC   Dialog, STN
> Compendex, Engineering Index.
> general engineering and technology

ERIC Document Reproduction Service. Springfield, VA   Dialog
> ERIC, Current Journals/Reports in Education.
> education

Global Engineering Documents. Irvine, CA   Dialog
> government and industry specifications and standards

GPO Publications Reference File. U.S. Government Printing Office,
Washington, DC   Dialog, GPO PRF
> U.S. government publications (not technical reports)

IFI/Plenum Data Co. Alexandria VA   Dialog
    Claims
    U.S. and non-U.S. patents
Information Store. San Francisco   Dialog
    any publicly available information
Institute for Scientific Information (ISI). The Genuine
Article (TGA). Philadelphia   Dialog, STN
    Science Citation Index; Social Science Citation
    Index; Arts & Humanities Citation Index; Current Contents.
    general periodical literature
National Technical Information Service (NTIS).
Springfield, VA   Dialog, STN
    NTIS; Government Reports Announcements & Index.
    government-sponsored research, technical reports,
    federal agency reports
Rapra Technology Ltd., UK   Dialog, STN
    Rapra Abstracts.
    plastics, rubber, polymer technology
Russian National Public Library for Science and
Technology (NTB). Document Supply Centre. Moscow   STN
University Microfilms International (UMI).
Ann Arbor, MI   Dialog, STN
    Dissertation Abstracts International.
    theses and dissertations; other subject databases;
general periodicals

T. Renee Daulong
Information Resource Services, Inc.
Austin, Texas
512-320-8354

3. Outsourcing and the Electronic Library

- Budget cuts.
- Staff cuts.
- Head count.
- Space limitations.
- Skyrocketing cost of materials.
- Staying abreast of new technologies.

These are all problems today's librarian must face. Many librarians are dealing with these problems through outsourcing. Outsourcing is the contracting out of services traditionally provided by library staff. Some examples of services that are being outsourced include document delivery and library functions such as shelving and journal check-in. This growing trend toward outsourcing is creating a new market niche for companies providing library support services, even with the advent of the electronic library.

Traditional Services

Some library functions such as document delivery have traditionally been outsourced to some extent. If a library patron needed an article from a journal not held in-house, a request would be sent to an interlibrary loan (ILL) service or to a company specializing in article reprints. Today, many companies are relying more on outsourcing document delivery and less on their own holdings. Budget cuts, skyrocketing journal and book costs, staff cuts, copyright issues, and space limitations are making it necessary to send more requests for article reprints to outside vendors rather than filling them in-house or having a runner to access local collections.

Some corporate libraries have taken this one step further. They are contracting out *all* document delivery functions. These libraries contract with an outside vendor to:

- track requests
- find appropriate sources to fill document requests
- fill requests from the library's in-house collection
- deliver articles directly to library patrons via interoffice mail
- generate statistics for document delivery, such as departmental chargebacks and turnaround time by vendor.

Outsourcing this function allows library staff to handle more pressing responsibilities. This type of service eliminates much of the time spent doing purely clerical work, such as tracking document orders and processing articles so they can be sent to patrons.

The document delivery function will be changing in another way in the electronic library. Without a doubt, electronic document delivery is the way of the future. As with all new technologies, there are a few bugs to work out first, though. Several vendors now have electronic ordering with delivery directly to your fax. This system works well in that turnaround time can be reduced dramatically. If an image of a document is already stored, the document can be delivered to the library in a matter of hours. However, a fax copy may not be the answer for scientific and engineering articles that contain detailed graphs or photos that must be free from distortion. Furthermore, if a library has a large number of article requests per month, a dedicated fax would be required. Clerical work is not necessarily reduced either. The current vendors require that each article be ordered individually (i.e., the librarian is essentially performing an on-line verification for *each* article request rather than just submitting a list of citations).

The second, and perhaps most important, new technology that will revolutionize electronic document delivery is the use of the Internet and other networks. Documents can be delivered directly to the librarian's computer, again, in a very short time. This technology is still in its infancy, however. Before this method can be fully utilized, a new method for storing graphic images must be devised. The creation of graphic images requires huge amounts of storage capacity. Furthermore, as above, scientists and engineers need copies of very detailed graphs and photos that are clear and exact; distortion created when scanning or printing the image cannot be tolerated. Additionally, industry standards have yet to be developed for the electronic document delivery. For example, each vendor currently offering document delivery through the Internet has its own software for receiving and processing the image. Does this mean that a librarian will need software with different user interfaces and procedures for every document delivery vendor? This would only add to the clerical work. Other issues related to electronic document delivery concern copyright and data integrity. It is fairly easy to make a photocopy of an article for other people now, but it will only get easier if you do not even need to leave your desk; just forward copies of your electronic document to your colleagues through E-mail. Such actions are in clear violation of the copyright laws. Furthermore, it is very easy to alter electronic documents and forward them on to others. These very important issues must be addressed before electronic document delivery can become the norm.

Understaffed and one-person libraries are turning to outside suppliers to handle other traditional duties as well. Contractors are paid to come in on a regular or an as-needed basis to shelve, file, or check in materials. This type of clerical work is very time-consuming. Yet it must be performed in a timely manner. It is difficult to explain to a patron that the current issue of his favorite journal is sitting in a three-foot-tall stack you haven't gotten to yet. By contracting out the clerical duties, library staff are then available for performing professional duties such as reference and on-line searching.

The role of outside vendors can be further expanded to that of "Library Sitter." In this function, a contractor is brought in to staff the library for a limited period of time while the librarians attend meetings or conferences, are on vacation or are sick, etc. This is more difficult to coordinate because it requires the contractor have an adequate knowledge of library procedures, the collection, the internal library processes, and the library staff. Several companies have found this service to be important in maintaining patron satisfaction and a desired level of service. It is a very valuable service with many advantages over the alternatives of having a "temp" with little library experience or leaving the library unstaffed. Closing the library or having it staffed by a temporary who has no knowledge of the library can be quite detrimental, particularly now that librarians are fighting to maintain budgets. Patrons expect professional service at all times. Turning patrons away or leaving them with the feeling that the service left something to be desired will be a major problem at budget time. It is usually the frustrations that patrons remember, rather than the successes.

Nontraditional Services

Library service companies are in a unique position. In addition to the traditional services mentioned above, these companies can take advantage of their position to offer nontraditional services such as acting as liaison between local clients.

My company seeks to facilitate communications and cooperation between local librarians. We have a broad base of contacts that are usually willing to help out a fellow librarian. For example, we use the collections of our clients to fill occasional article requests made by other local librarians. We help our clients get information ASAP by acting as a go-between among clients. Why wait weeks and pay big dollars for something if you can borrow it from someone down the road this afternoon? We facilitate information exchange between corporate libraries as well as between corporate and academic librarians. Clients frequently ask how other clients have handled similar situations. We are also called upon to take discards from one library to another or asked if we know who could use this or that item. As budgets and collections diminish, cooperation among neighbors is becoming increasingly important.

We also try to keep librarians up to date with current developments that affect both our company and theirs. Such issues include copyright, the document delivery business, and developments at the libraries we use as document delivery sources. We provide a different perspective that may help our clients see the big picture.

Another unique service our company offers is giving tours of the University of Texas Libraries. These libraries are accessible to the general public, a fact many people do not realize. This library tour service has had tremendous success. Close to 100 employees of one local company have gone on tours, including all of their corporate library staff. We have nearly a decade of experience in these libraries and are able to show what kind of information is, and is not, available from this tremendous collection. It gives our clients a better feel for the costs and time constraints of our document delivery service. The tours are tailored to demonstrate the similarities and differences between the academic library and their own corporate library. It lets the patron see the wealth of information that is available locally. As we walk through the stacks, they also discover sources of information that they may not have known about. We suggest that a representative from the corporate library always attend the tour. This allows her to get to know her patrons in a more casual setting, to find out what types of information they are interested in, and to discover ways to provide better service to her patrons. The librarian can also explain which sources are available in-house and why others are not. People who go on these tours usually become much more active users of their own corporate library.

We also use the tours as a chance to educate library patrons about the cost of information. It is a great way to educate them in an informal, low-pressure situation. A casual, anecdotal conversation about the restrictions on photocopying due to the Copyright Act seems to be remembered more easily and have more impact. We explain that it is not legal for them to copy an article that they wrote from a journal their library subscribes to without paying additional royalties to the publisher. We also chat about the skyrocketing cost of journals and explain that this is why most collections, both academic and corporate, are shrinking rapidly. By pointing out journals that cost up to $6,000 per year, we show that this is why their library may not subscribe to their favorite journal.

The Successful Library Service Company

Today, library service companies have a tremendous opportunity. The unfortunate fact is that downsizing is in, and many of the cuts are hitting libraries particularly hard. Librarians are turning to outsourcing to make up for staff and budget cuts. Library service companies can take advantage of this trend. But these companies must have some underlying principles if they are to succeed. Customer satisfaction, fast turnaround, personalized service, and flexibility are keys to success.

Customer satisfaction is extremely important for library service companies. Librarians are great at networking. The recommendation of satisfied clients is the best marketing tool available. Conversely, upset clients can quickly ruin your business. It is important always to go that extra mile to ensure client satisfaction.

Fast turnaround time is crucial. A library service company must be able to respond quickly. Services that are outsourced tend to be those that have sat around until they became urgent. The piles of loose-leaf filing must be filed today. The piles of journals must be checked in and shelved today. The patron needed his article yesterday. A quick response means a happy customer. A slow response means that customer is lost.

Personalized, friendly service is also required. The contractor must have an adequate knowledge and understanding of each client's specific needs in order to be effective. He must be seen as a coworker or colleague, rather than an outside vendor; one of "us" rather than one of "them."

Flexibility is critical. Our clients continually push us to offer more services. Some of these, such as the library tours, are very innovative. Our official motto is "If it isn't illegal and we can figure out how to bill you for it, we can do it." It is an amusing motto, but it really has a deeper underlying meaning. As all of today's management gurus are telling us, if you are not creative and flexible, you will not survive.

Summary

Technological and philosophical changes are driving libraries into the electronic age. Electronic document delivery and access to new sources of information through the Internet will have a dramatic impact on the traditional library. Yet changes in the philosophy of business will also have a large impact. As companies downsize, budgets and staffs will be reduced. While the new technologies may ease some of the strains created by smaller staffs, they are not necessarily *the* answer. Many of the technologies will have clerical work associated with them, such as processing and delivering electronic documents to patrons. Furthermore, the paper journal will not disappear for a long time. Someone will still need to check journals in and shelve them. Finally, electronic technology changes at a very rapid pace. Librarians will have to work constantly to stay abreast of new developments. All these factors suggest that outsourcing may play an important role in the electronic library.

III. CREATING THE TRUE ELECTRONIC LIBRARY--LANs AND THE INTERNET

Many prognosticators and dreamers believe that networking and the Internet are just the vanguard of technologies that will transform libraries and information centers into true electronic libraries. While LANs (local area networks) and the Internet may be the wave of the future, the fact is that OPAC (on-line public-access catalogs) and electronic circulation are the real foundations of the "library without walls." These systems have become so common that many users don't remember what it was like before automated circulation and MARC cataloging made it possible for libraries and vendors to build OPACs. And the development of OPACs has made it possible for Internet users to look at library catalogs around the world without paying for long distance telephone calls. Sadly, though the catalogs of some fairly large libraries and most corporate librarie cannot be accessed via telephone dial-up, much less the Internet.

If networks are the next step into the future, then we all need to know more about LANs and the Internet. The next chapter, by William Kopplin and Molly White, is just the place to start, because it provides an overview of networking, including how a network works, an extensive glossary of terms, and a checklist to aid in assessing a library's need for a network

In the second chapter in this section, "Casting the Internet," Jo Anne Newyear talks about the technology that has the potential to interconnect every library and workplace. Although the total interconnection of every computer on every desk may not happen with the Internet, it is a giant step forward toward creating the true electronic library. This chapter ends with selected copies of handouts from user education classes at UT. These will give you an idea of how a large university library is helping its undergraduates access the information they need to be successful in their studies.

William Kopplin
Computer Sciences Librarian,
LLWJK@utxdp.dp.utexas.edu
Molly White
Physics Mathematics Astronomy Librarian
LLMTW@utxdp.dp.utexas.edu
The General Libraries
The University of Texas at Austin

4. LANs — Networking the Computers in Your Organization

Libraries are operating in an increasingly complex technical environment. Many libraries are merging with management information systems departments within their organizations, and they are using computers for everything from database maintenance to word processing to purchasing to label-making. In any fiscal environment it is necessary to maximize the use of computing resources. One way to better utilize computing power is to link machines together into a network.

A LAN (local area network) is a system of computers in close proximity joined together. It can be as simple as two computers cabled together, or it can be as complex as groups of computers linked to mainframes and other networks.

All information professionals who work with computers need to know about the power to be gained by linking computers into a system. A LAN can increase your productivity by letting you share software and peripheral equipment such as printers. A LAN can increase your communication capabilities through E-mail, and most important, a LAN can help you deliver information to your users.

If you are a member of one of the 75 percent of corporations that are currently implementing LANs, you should plan to link your library to the system and increase your visibility. And if your library is already fully connected to your organization, you can explore the advantages to be gained through global connectivity (see the Internet chapter). You can gain very valuable basic services through networking.

E-mail

Communication is improved through E-mail (electronic mail) in numerous ways. E-mail is fast and can help reduce paper clutter. E-mail communications can easily range from the very informal and personal to the official and archival. It saves "phone tag" irritations and facilitates group work. Most E-mail systems provide for electronic filing and searching of documents and messages. Increased access to information and improved communications are strategic advantages in any organization.

Calendar scheduling software is another feature of E-mail that enhances communications among working groups. Meetings, training sessions, and other activities are easily coordinated with calendar software.

Software Sharing

Networks allow for the sharing of the most recent versions of programs. It is easy to install updates and thus ensure uniformity in software usage. Most software packages are sold in single-user versions and multi-user network versions. The network versions are priced to make it more economical to extend usage to several users rather than purchasing individual copies of software. This practice is called site licensing and can save money. With a network in place, everyone in a company can use the same version of a program — i.e., word processing, accounting, database management, etc. Files can be shared easily, and levels of access can be controlled from a central point.

The central control point also helps companies prove they are not making illegal copies of software. Special LAN software exists that allows administrators to monitor the distribution of software applications electronically.

Another advantage that a LAN can provide is the automatic back-up of files and systems. System control software can be set so that back-ups are frequent and automatic, thus freeing the individual program users from attempting to remember to secure their work.

Peripherals

One important motivation for most organizations in setting up a computer network is printer sharing. High-quality laser printers are expensive, and with a network in place, several users can direct their printing to a single piece of equipment. This spreads the expense over the entire network and makes it feasible to purchase top-performing equipment.

The same rationale applies to other hardware as well. Modems, fax boards, back-up devices, and CD-ROM drives can all be networked to system users. Network users also gain access to other hard drives and can utilize extra file space if needed. A computer network spreads equipment costs among many users.

Security

A network allows a company to control information access privileges. For instance, only certain people should have access to payroll records, but all employees should be able to view policy documents. A network allows data and information to be shared widely while it also enables access to sensitive information to be restricted. Also, the ability to modify and erase information can be limited to certain users while allowing others to view the same files.

Access privileges are usually controlled by log-on procedures and passwords. A network manager usually administers the security functions and designs directories and menus that facilitate access to commonly available files while restricting access to the operating system and to sensitive documents or applications.

Library Connection

A LAN is a tool that can enhance a library's ability to provide services to its clientele. Do you have databases to share with your organization- - on-line catalogs, lists of journal holdings, data files? Do you need to promote your services to your clients? Would it improve your delivery of services to be able to send search results electronically, to scan and fax answers to reference questions via E-mail, to communicate directly with the research staff in your organization, or to route messages to several people at once? Have you invested in a CD-ROM product that your users would like to access from their offices?

A linked computer system is a powerful tool that is used in myriad ways in all types of libraries. It is a dynamic tool whose uses will expand once a system is installed and operational. The library can carve a niche in training network users. Network managers are often technically focused. The service orientation of libraries can be an opportunity to expand your base of operations and to prove your usefulness to management by providing user-friendly training.

Survey and evaluate the computing functions in your organization. Perhaps you need to build a LAN to connect personnel and functions within the library. If you want to connect to an existing company LAN outside the library, you should immediately start talking with the systems manager. Or perhaps you already are networked and simply want to connect with a larger network. In any case, do your homework and gather information to support your proposal.

Assessing Your Needs

Before contemplating or purchasing any equipment, assess your current needs and problems to determine if a LAN could help your organization. Are you in a computer-intensive environment? Are there problems you need to solve? The following checklist can help guide your thinking as you build your case.

"Need a Network?" Checklist
1. List the resources you need to share among users:
   A. Printers:
   B. Disk space:
   C. Fax boards:
   D. Modems:
   E. CD-ROM drives:
   F. Other:
2. Do users frequently exchange disks containing data files?
3. Do users need to use the same data files?
4. Would you like to pass messages to each other without walking to each office or desk?
5. Do you have a system powerful enough (at least a 286) to function as the main server for printing and file sharing? If not, will you buy one?
6. Are the workstations on the same floor, with a suspended ceiling to run the network cables?
7. Can you afford to spend fro $200-$400 per workstation?
8. Do you have the extra time required to design and manage the network?
9. Are you ready to handle the new problems created by the network?
10. Do you have someone who can provide help when you need it?

Derrick, Dan. 1992. *Network Know-How: Concepts, Cards & Cables.* Osborne McGraw-Hill, pp. 12-13. [used with permission]

We will review some points in Derrick's checklist.
1. Resources:
   A. Printers. Printers are commonly used on networks.
   Check their location to minimize user travel distance
   and the need for special paper insertion. The printer is
   likely to wear out quickly. If your only reason to
   network is to link two computers to a laser printer, you
   might want to investigate the use of an inexpensive T-
   switch. A T-switch is a simple electrical toggle switch
   that allows you to control the direction of your output.
   B. Disk space. Hard disks are also commonly used on
   networks. Disk storage space and hard drive space can
   be increased. This is not cost-effective if it is the only
   reason to network. Beware of the disadvantages of
   having important files stored in only one place. In case
   of failure, all the users of the files are at risk.
   C. Fax boards. Networked fax boards are a handy way
   to communicate with other parts of the world. They can
   save time if your fax machine is used frequently. It is
   difficult to fax anything from a fax board if it does not
   originate from the computer.
   D. Modems. If users rely on telecommunication links
   with outside sources, access to a modem through a
   network is possible.
   E. CD-ROM drives. Many libraries purchase
   information in a CD-ROM format. Review your
   licensing agreement to make sure your version is
   authorized for network use. Investigate the costs
   associated with obtaining site licenses for CD-ROMs.
   F. Other. Many computer users store or back up data on
   tape drives. These could also be accessible via a
   network. Scanners are another example of costly
   equipment that can be shared. The output from a
   scanner can be easily sent to any networked workstation.
2. Are you transferring files between computers by carrying disks
   to the office that needs the information?
3. Do several users need to access, update, or modify the same
   files? Is your organization arranged into workgroups spread
   over different locations with several people working on the
   same project?
4. E-mail can become a new and important channel of
   communications, especially when consistent use is established.
   Calendar scheduling software is available to coordinate meetings.
   When used properly, E-mail can be a step toward paperwork
   reduction.

5. Do you have a computer powerful enough (4 MB memory, hard drive larger than 80 MB) to function as the main server for printing and file sharing? If not, will you buy one? These days, a 286 chip is no longer adequate, and even a 386 is usually not recommended. You may as well go all the way up to a 486 chip or equivalent for a DOS machine. If you plan on using an Apple computer or other non-DOS computer as your server, you should also make sure it uses a high-powered chip.
6. Inspect your surroundings for features that would ease the task of stringing cable between machines. Suspended ceilings help, as does an existing chase or conduit that can be used to run cable.
7. Costs can vary even more than $200 to $400 to modify existing equipment, depending on exact network features.
8. Does anyone in your organization have the expertise required to plan and/or manage a network? Will you be able to hire a consultant or more staff if necessary to handle network demands?
9. Is your organization flexible enough to cope with new problems? Networks bring increased complexity, more things to break, program conflicts.
10. Is there someone on staff or available as a consultant who can help when inevitable problems arise? You need to plan for downtime, equipment and software backups, disasters, etc.

Problems that LANs *won't* solve:
- Security. A LAN usually creates more security problems than it eliminates.
- Universal exchange of information and data. File format incompatibilities will still exist and may even be exaggerated.
- Administration. LANs add another layer of complexity to both the equipment and the personnel.
- Large databases. A LAN server may not be powerful enough to handle a really large database.

Technical Considerations

Most companies decide to install a LAN because they already have a major investment in equipment. Tying existing computers together allows each computer to retain its ability to work as an independent personal computer running its own software as well as to assume new duties as a network workstation with access to all other resources, programs, and files. Three things are usually required to transform independent computers into a network: special networking software, a special interface card (most often a circuit board that plugs into one of the computer's expansion slots) for each machine, and cables that physically link all the components together (there are also wireless LANs that use various wireless transmitting technologies to allow for the necessary network communication).

These three things are all off-the-shelf pieces of equipment that can be purchased at most computer dealers and retailers. Especially when dealing with small networks, you can almost go to the store, buy the pieces, and install the network yourself. But first let's discuss networks in the abstract. This will help you evaluate the claims of salespeople and the advice of consultants and helpful bystanders.

TYPES OF NETWORKS

There are two basic types of LANs: client-server networks and peer-to-peer networks. Both types are popular and effective and you need to understand the differences between them before you can start making decisions. It should be noted, though, that there are also hybrid systems where the network software will let a workstation act as a peer or, alternatively, as a client-server.

Peer-to-Peer

Peer-to-peer LANs are ideal for small simple networks. All computer workstations are considered to be equal, and all network resources (printers, hard disk drives, etc.) can be shared. Each workstation is directly connected to all other workstations and can send files to and receive files from any other workstation on the network. These systems are sometimes called *distributed-server networks,* since no one central server exists--each worstation acts somewhat as a server to all the others. The computers on peer-to-peer networks can be thought of as co-workers in an flat organization with no administrative hierarchy.

The network operating software for peer-to-peer LANs is generally less expensive and easier in install, operate, and maintain than the software for client-server LANs. The software is designed and marketed for smaller organizations, which may not have large information systems offices capable of lending technical support. LANtastic is one of the best-known brands of network software for peer-to-peer LANs. One advantage of this type of network is that, many times, off-the-shelf application packages that aren't LAN-aware will still function normally.

Slotless networks are a special set of peer-to-peer networks. Slotless LANs, also referred to as zero-slot LANs, consist of computers linked together with cables only. In all other networks, in addition to the cables, it is necessary to add a network interface card (NIC) to one of the internal expansion slots in each networked computer. The only advantage a slotless network offers is that some computers don't have very many slots and a slotless LAN will save those very valuable expansion ports for other purposes.

A slotless network works like all other peer-to-peer networks with all communication between computers being handled by ordinary serial cable, which is normally used to attach peripheral equipment such as printers. Slotless networks are very inexpensive and limited to a handful of computers in close proximity to each other. They have no growth potential and are not recommended for anything but the most basic networks.

> Caution: Some computers use cable connectors with the same number of pins for different purposes. Sometimes the only difference between parallel and serial ports is the gender of the plug. Thus it is possible to accidentally connect one computer's serial port to another computer's parallel port. Don't do this. This can damage your computer.

Client-Server

As peer-to-peer networks grow larger, the computing load for the networked equipment grows more complex, and for that reason, the most popular type of network for medium to large networks, or for any networks that may one day be medium to large, is the client-server network. In client-server LANs, networked computer workstations are not equal. They are divided into two groups: the clients or users — that is, you and your fellow employees sitting at desks using computers, and the server, which interacts with you and makes its resources available whenever you need any network services. Network services can include communicating with other workstations, communicating with co-workers through E-mail, accessing remote or shared files and databases, storing or backing up files you may not want to store on your workstation, printing, etc.

THE SERVER

One computer is usually assigned the role of the network disk server or file server (the server, for short). The software that runs the server forms a shell around the server's operating system (typically DOS), filtering out commands sent to the machine before DOS can receive them.

The software maintains an inventory, known as the file allocation table (FAT), that keeps track of where particular files are stored. The server thus acts as a "waitperson" (hence "server") filling the order of a remote workstation on the network, a "customer," for some sort of file. The server delivers the file to the workstation, or "table," of the client, or customer. The file requests can be handled by direct commands or by selecting items from an on-screen menu.

Small networks can usually be supported by a single centralized server. To remain efficient, larger networks often use multiple servers. For example, one server may be in the accounting office area with accounting files on it, another server may be in the personnel office area with personnel files on it, and so on. This arrangement speeds up network performance and can expedite certain duties like making backup copies of files. Multiple servers also mean that if one server becomes inoperative, the whole LAN is not necessarily shut down. Network security, however, can become much more complex with these larger client-server LANs.

The computer operating as the network server can be either dedicated, that is, it operates only as a server and you can't do anything else with it, or nondedicated, which means you can still use it as a regular computer. Nondedicated file server systems are thus often less expensive (there is no need to buy or set aside a whole computer) but they are also often slower. This can be a false economy. The time lost by all the users on all the network workstations adds up. Generally, centralized file servers should be dedicated if you have a network with more than five or six workstations. The more powerful the server is, the better. This is one case where you should buy as much computer as you can afford.

SPECIALIZED SERVERS

A print server is a special type of server designed to share printers. Heavy-duty printing requirements or the use of specialized printers, such as plotters, suggest the use of dedicated network printers with their own network interface cards (NICs). The use of a print server is almost essential in situations where there is routine printing of large files, which would otherwise congest network traffic. The server manages the printers and queues up the incoming print jobs assigned to them.

In libraries, CD-ROM servers are becoming more and more popular. A CD-ROM server manages CD-ROMs, much as a print server manages printers, by queuing the requests for CD-ROM access. Thus all the workstations in the network have access to the various databases stored on the networked CD-ROM drives. The CD-ROM server manages the administrative details of responding to the commands sent by the individual workstations.

There are other specialized servers for certain situations. Storage servers can handle various types of data storage systems such as tape drives, Bernoulli boxes (removable data storage cartridges), and networked hard drives. This type of server is often used when large amounts of automated backups need to be made or when very large databases need to be shared. And video servers can manage specialized video equipment and peripherals, such as VCRs, etc.

Topology, or How a Network Is Laid Out

Topology refers to the physical design and layout of the network. Three popular topologies are: star, bus, and token-ring The star topology has the server in the center. The networked workstations communicate through the server. If a workstation fails, the network is unaffected, but if the server fails, the whole network goes down. This is very similar to the way the phone system works. A broken phone on your desk won't bring the whole system down, but a system accident can sure keep your phone from working. Star typologies are often seen on Ethernet or older STARLAN or ARCnet networks.

The star topology offers at least three advantages: (1) additional workstations are very easy to install; (2) the central server can often assign a higher status to selected workstations (this is useful if some users require faster response time than others), and (3) centralized diagnostics of all network functions are very easily accomplished.

The bus topology is simply a long single connection with workstations attached to it. It is similar to a street with several houses on it, the cars pulling into and out of the garages metaphorically being the messages passed between workstations. A system known as carrier sense multiple access with collision detection (CSMA/CD) was developed to keep the cars from running into each other. Bus systems can be either peer-to-peer or client-server. Bus systems are often found on Ethernet and Novell networks.

The bus topology also offers at least three advantages: (1) cable requirements are very simple, bus networks use less cable than any other kind, and it can often be low-cost twisted-pair cabling; (2) it is easy to add new workstations to systems with a dedicated server or to peer-to-peer systems; and (3) when one workstation fails, the rest of the network can remain operational. One disadvantage is that bus topologies have fewer inherent security features than star topologies. Thus it is easier for an unauthorized user to gain access to the network.

The third topology is token-ring, in which the ends of the above-mentioned street are connected together to form a ring. The network messages ("cars") avoid collisions due to the "electronic tokens" the network software creates (tokens can also sometimes be used with bus topologies). Token-Ring used as a brandname refers to the proprietary system developed by IBM.

A token-ring topology is often strong enough to withstand the failures of multiple workstations, since inoperative workstations can simply be bypassed. The token-monitoring workstation that handles diagnostic functions can also be easily reassigned. New workstations can be added only either while the network is shut down or through the use of special connectors called wire centers.

In addition to these three main topologies, there are also a couple of lesser known, more specialized ones: the loop, which is sometimes prone to performance problems and system crashes, and the tree, which is really just a complex bus, or a series of buses arranged in a hierarchical manner. Mixed topologies are also used occasionally, such as a star-ring arrangement. And some writers refer to the different topologies with different terminology, so don't worry too much if you get confused.

LAN Cabling

Now that you have given thought to what type of network you need and what topology would be best, you should consider what kind of cabling to use. LAN cabling is the physical medium needed to link the individual workstations together with the server and all the peripheral equipment. The three main types are twisted-pair, coaxial (co-ax), and fiber-optic, and each type has advantages and disadvantages. Since there is a considerable range in cable cost and capability, cabling is not a trivial matter, though by itself the cable is one of the less expensive pieces of network equipment. If a network is already in place and you are simply interested in getting connected to it, you should probably use the same cable as the rest of the network. If you are building a new network, you should look at the physical requirements of your office and your plans for the future growth of the LAN.

Check to see which types of cables are supported by the brands of network software (Novell, LANtastic, etc.) and the associated network interface cards you are considering and then check to be sure the cables are capable of operating over the distances between the workstations you want to network. Choose a cable type that will be capable of handling your future needs.

BANDWIDTH

Before examining the three types of cable, we need to discuss bandwidth. Bandwidth is the measure of how much information can be carried by the network cable. To a network designer faced with transmitting a large amount of data, bandwidth is everything — the more the better. In the context of LANs, there are two flavors of bandwidth, *baseband* and *broadband.*

Baseband is a technique for transmitting signals (the electric pulses carrying the coded information) over cables where the signal is placed directly on the cable in digital form without any type of modulation. Baseband can be likened to two coffee cans tied together by string. The string isn't strictly digital, but you get the picture. Baseband is one-channel communication and is direct, simple, cheap, and proven. Most small LANs use baseband primarily because of the cost and the fact that usable twisted-pair (phone wire) cable is so readily available. However, baseband is limited in how far signals can be sent — usually no more than a couple of miles.

Broadband is an analog technique for transmitting signals where the signal is modulated and thus capable of carrying significantly more information. The modulation places different signals into different frequencies so that there can be multiple channels in the transmission each capable of carrying voice, data, video, etc. Broadband can be likened to two coffee cans tied together by string and wire and phone cord and TV cable, and so on.

Broadband is always used for larger networks and whenever voice and data (and other signals) are so numerous that they need to be sent simultaneously. Broadband transmissions can be made over much greater distances and they can operate at very high speeds; consequently, much more information can be communicated. With this increase in scale, in both speed and capacity, comes an increase in complexity, so broadband systems often require more specialized support equipment that is sometimes best left to the experts to handle.

CABLE TYPES

Now that you know how to measure the performance of cable-- baseband for normal LAN performance and broadband for high performance--you can think about the different physical types of cable. The two types of networks and the different topologies discussed above can operate over any of the cable types summarized in the accompanying chart.

LAN Cabling Basics

	Twisted-pair wire	Baseband coaxial cable	Broadband coaxial cable	Fiber-optic cable
Topology	Bus, star or star	Bus or ring	Bus or Ring	Bus, Ring, or star
Channels	Single	Single	Multiple	Single or multiple
Speed	2 - 16 Mbps	2 - 100 Mbps	As high as 400 Mbps	As high as Gbps
Distance Apart	1000s of feet	Miles	10s of miles	10s of miles
Number of networked computers	250 or less	1000 or less	1000s	1000s
Advantages	Low cost; can use existing wiring	Low cost; simple to install	Can handle voice, data, and video	Can handle voice, data, and video
Disadvantages	Limited capability may need conduits; subject to interference	Subject to interference	High cost; requires special equipment	High cost; dificult to splice

Twisted-pair

Twisted-pair cable, sometimes referred to as phone wire, is really a family of similarly constructed wire offered in a wide variety of grades and qualities. Twisted-pair is inherently baseband, so the amount of information it can carry is limited. The main advantage to twisted-pair cable is that it is the least expensive type. Twisted-pair consists of two insulated wires twisted together so that electrical interference from the surrounding environment is minimized. This interference, or "noise," would contaminate the network signal if the wires weren't twisted. Smaller LANs often use very inexpensive unshielded twisted-pair telephone cable. For example, IBM supports unshielded telephone wire in its Token-Ring Network. Generally, the higher the grade of wire, the better the data transmission quality can be maintained over long distances.

Coaxial

The original coaxial cable ("frozen garden hose") was large, thick, expensive, stiff, and relatively difficult to work with. Many of these problems have now been resolved, and today's co-ax, particularly the simpler baseband co-ax, is almost as easy to work with as twisted-pair cabling. Co-ax and Ethernet are sometimes mistakenly used as synonyms. They refer to two different things, although there are thousands of Ethernet LANs running over co-ax cable, so the confusion is understandable.

ETHERNET

Ethernet, invented in 1973 by Robert Metcalfe while working at Xerox, is today the most popular network system, with an installed base approaching 25 million computers. In comparison, it is estimated that there are fewer than 10 million networked computers using any of the other major connection schemes—IBM's Token-Ring, LocalTalk, ARCnet, FDDI, etc. Based on IEEE 802.3 LAN specifications, Ethernet was originally developed by Xerox, Digital, and Intel, and it has now matured into a widely accepted standard supported by almost all manufacturers of networking equipment and software. Ethernet can be configured in several different ways. Ethernet using unshielded twisted-pair can implement a star topology. Ethernet using shielded coaxial cable, either thick or thin, can implement a bus topology. Ethernet employs CSMA/CD to ensure reliable transmission. CSMA/CD can be compared to a group of people at a very long table in a restaurant who are very polite and always wait and listen to see if anyone else is talking before they say anything.

A standard for very high speed Ethernet is currently being drafted. This development, combined with falling prices for Ethernet adapter cards, ensures the viability of Ethernet networks well into the future. A word of caution: while Ethernet was designed to be a standard, there is, paradoxically, no standard Ethernet. Thus Ethernet products from different manufacturers may not work with each other. Carefully investigate the specifications of Ethernet products before deciding if they will be compatible with your other network equipment.

Fiber-optic

Fiber-optic refers to the fact that the coded signal is sent via a beam of light rather than an electrical charge as in twisted-pair or coaxial cable. Fiber-optic cable offers several advantages over the other two cable types. It offers much higher data transmission speeds, it is more immune to electrical interference, and it can span much greater distances. Fiber-optic cable is inherently broadband, so its capabilities may be unnecessary for smaller LANs. At present, fiber-optic cable and its associated connectors are relatively expensive, although with the increasing use of fiber-optic cable in the telecommunications industry, prices are decreasing.

Additional LAN Features

Occasionally, the unique characteristics of an office environment require a wireless LAN. An example is an office with asbestos in the ceiling that shouldn't be disturbed, or an office where the network equipment is constantly being rearranged, thus making it desirable to avoid repeated rewiring. Not having to install cables makes building the network easier, and it brings with it a great deal of flexibility.

A wireless LAN works like any other LAN, but instead of cables running between computers, the signals are transmitted by one of two wireless methods: radio waves or infrared beams.

Infrared systems work like very sophisticated TV remote controls. The infrared signals can span hundreds of feet, but they can't go through walls or floors. They can go over low walls or dividers because the infrared receiver/transmitters are placed on elevated poles. Thus these systems are limited to environments where the various pieces of networked equipment are in sight of each other.

Systems using radio waves can span greater distances than infrared systems and can penetrate most walls. Equipment prices for both types of wireless systems are dropping as more manufacturers like Hewlett-Packard and others enter the business. Standards in this area are currently being negotiated and experts believe that wireless LANs will become even more popular in the future. It is assumed that the FCC will reserve certain very high radio frequencies specifically for use in wireless networks.

The whole idea behind LANs is connection. No sooner is a LAN up and running than users want to connect it to other resources — additional databases, other LANs, WANs (wide-area networks), and so on. The concept of internetworking has become very popular in the last few years, and numerous mechanisms, known as gateways, by which LANs can be connected to other computers, are now available. Within an organization, similar LANs can be connected to each other via simple bridges. Dissimilar LANs, or LANs and WANs, can be connected with routers that are capable of overcoming the incompatibilities between networks. When the scale of internetwork traffic becomes large enough, or complex enough, a gateway machine, a special processor or computer dedicated to this function, may be necessary to adequately handle the load.

IBM, as the dominant producer of large mainframe computers, has released or supported a wide range of products designed to help LANs make connections with mainframes. Since mainframes have traditionally run proprietary operating systems, there are inherently more incompatibilities when a mainframe is included as a node in a network. IBM's SNA (Systems Network Architecture) is a collection of protocols and specifications that ease the connection process and help transfer some of the mainframe's computational power to the individual user. Other solutions are available for machines from other manufacturers; for example, Digital has designed DECnet as a way to connect office computers to Digital mainframes such as PDPs and VAXes.

Connecting LANs to other equipment, such as mainframes, is a whole sub-industry in itself, one that is full of acronyms and buzzwords like *downsizing* (converting mainframe functions to LANs) and *rightsizing* (placing the appropriate application on the appropriate machine). Don't be discouraged. Ask around and find others in the same boat. Look for topical electronic bulletin boards and newsgroups on the Internet.

Planning a Network

Once you have decided to install a network and have acquired an understanding of the technical issues, it is time to plan the network. Key components to be considered are the equipment and software on hand, a survey of the needs of potential network participants, the physical layout of the spaces to be included in the network, and measurements of the distances between workstations.

User needs: What programs are used, and what applications are needed via network access? How much memory is required for the networked versions of those programs? What are your total storage requirements, and what type of printing or other peripheral access is required?

Existing equipment: How much memory is available? Are the right slots available for the appropriate network interface cards? What types of display are in use or will need to be supported? These issues need to be very carefully checked. Pay close attention to such details as the exact specification of slots and connectors.

New equipment: Is there a need for computer or memory upgrades? What additional peripheral equipment (printers, CD-ROM drives, etc.) needs to be purchased? What will be needed in future expansions?

Software requirements: Is there a network version of your existing applications software? How much does the network version cost per workstation?   Which LAN software supports your applications?

E-mail requirements: What E-mail services are your users going to need? Are links to other mail systems necessary? Do you need immediate notification of incoming mail messages? This type of notification will require more memory. Do you need to attach files to E-mail messages? Do you need your E-mail system to be linked to other packages, such as calendar scheduling software? There is a variety of E-mail packages offered by the major vendors. Read the fine print.

File configuration: Are all programs and files going to be stored and used on the network (similar to a mainframe computer operation)? Or are all programs and files going to be stored on the local workstations, with the network to be used only to connect to peripherals? Or will the system consist of a mix of those two options?

Choose the type of network (and hence network software) to be installed:

- Slotless networks connect through the serial ports of from 2 to 4 computers. Networking software and cards are very inexpensive.
- Peer-to-peer networks require software and network cards to be purchased for each station on the network. Two examples of network operating software for peer-to-peer systems are Artisoft's LANtastic and Novell's NetWare Lite.
- Client-server networks utilize one computer to run the network. Software is more complicated, and software prices are determined by the number of users. Two examples of network operating software for this type of network are Novell's NetWare and Microsoft's LAN Manager.

Cable type: How far apart are the workstations? What restrictions are imposed by the walls or other physical or electrical considerations? Can you afford to install fiber-optic cable? Have you considered a wireless installation?

Platform compatibility: Most organizations support a variety of computer hardware and operating system platforms (i.e., DOS, Macintosh, UNIX, Windows, etc.). Will the network need to be able to handle multiple platforms? Will the network need to provide interoperability for users who use the same applications and services on different hardware and operating systems?

Network management: Who will manage the network? Who will design and install the network equipment and software? Will a consultant be hired? Will additional permanent staff be necessary?

Installation plan: Document the plan with schedules and calendars for all to share. Plan on everything taking twice as long as expected and troubleshoot the consequences of such delays. Don't rush the installation. Try to plan the work for a time when users are not using their applications.

Budget

The network plan forms the basis for a budget. Costs can vary from $400 per workstation on a small network to $2000-plus per workstation on a large, complex system.

Consult with others who have installed the systems you have under consideration. Read reviews of network hardware and software in computer magazines. Get on the mailing lists of the many free networking trade magazines and send for vendor brochures and catalogs. Attend users' group meetings in your area and ask participants about their LAN experiences. Computer bulletin boards (BBSes) can also be a source of information on systems and programs. Try to gather varied opinions and recommendations. Check and double-check vendor claims against what you've learned.

One good printed source on prices and related information is the Datapro series entitled *Managing LANs*. Datapro publishes an extensive series of titles, usually looseleaf binders with monthly updates. Datapro and its competitor Faulkner provide a wide range of valuable information on networks and other computer topics that is available in print, on disk, or in CD-ROM format. The reports are expensive, so try to find them in a local library first.

And remember this rule of thumb:

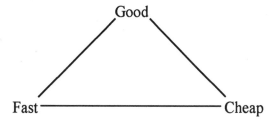

Pick any two corners. You can have any two attributes in a networking environment, but you cannot get all three.

Do-It-Yourself vs. Hiring a Consultant

If you have the time, expertise, and patience to tackle a large electronic project you can consider self-installation. The many self-help books in the computer section of most large bookstores offer guidance to computer-literate power users. Plan to buy wiring/cabling tools, ladders, and anything else needed to run cable and install cards in computer equipment.

Ask yourself these questions: Are you "hardware-literate" enough to handle the project? Do you routinely take the cover off your computer to install such things extra chips or memory and adapter cards for video drivers, performance extenders, or additional hard drives? Have you changed the switches and jumpers on such cards? Are you very familiar with the various types of cables and cable connectors, including video and telephone wires? Have you ever routed cable before? If you can answer yes to these questions, you may be a good candidate for installing your own network.

If you are a part of a company that already has computer support staff, you will find that cultivating their friendship and goodwill helps when installing a LAN. A sound working relationship with that department or staff member is crucial to the success of this or any other project. Good, open communication is necessary to maintain their support and cooperation throughout the process.

If you decide that self-installation or installation by your support staff is unworkable, the next step is to hire a computer consultant. Individuals as well as computer service companies will share expertise for payment. Fees are usually negotiable and can range from $35 to $100 per hour. Complete most of your research and planning before interviewing potential consultants. Decide what services you need — design?

purchase? installation? user training? Know your time frame — how soon do you need to have an operative system? What sort of experience and communication skills do you need?

To find a consultant you should ask for referrals from others, consult with members of users' groups, talk to computer dealers, and check the yellow pages. Find out if the job can be performed within your deadline. Ask for references and follow up with phone calls about the consultant's previous performance.

Ongoing support is a service you should also consider. Rare is the system or user who does not need outside help. You can consult the manual, try the help desk of the software company, and even send queries to electronic bulletin boards asking for help with your problems. When all else fails, you can pay your consultant by the hour for phone-in help or for a site visit.

Network Management

Every network needs a manager. Depending on the size and complexity of the system, the job can range from an hour a week to a full-time job with support staff. Remember this adage: Small systems demand attention. Large systems require FTEs.

The network manager is in charge of keeping the network operable and performs the following functions:

- Maintenance: Routine backup of files and data.
- Security: Designates access to files and sets up users with passwords and log-on IDs.
- Repair and troubleshooting: Tracks down errors and system failures. Keeps the network in good working order. Performs system checks and other support duties.
- Oversees proper usage: Keeps users from storing extraneous data on valuable network space. Tracks usage and shifts resources to accommodate use patterns. Gathers use data and prepares reports for planning future network developments.
- Training: Provides staff with ongoing training related to the use of application software in a networked environment. Provides initial training for all updates and new network services.

The best network manager is one with a service orientation whose goal is to make the network serve the needs of the users. This may seem obvious, but many organizations unfortunately make the mistake of allowing the technical needs of the network to constrain the users.

Training

Training is the key to success for any new endeavor. LAN training will be essential for all employees (including managers) whose work involves use of the system. E-mail training is basic to employee communications and should be a component of new employee education and orientation.

In-house training sessions are necessary to train current employees in the use of a new system. Provide handouts and be sure to include a one-sheet command summary for quick reference. Be sure to cover such issues as what to do in case of a system crash, how to report problems, handling issues of privacy, and E-mail etiquette. Users may have access to new applications and will need program-specific training. On-line tutorials, videotapes, and manuals are all helpful support mechanisms, but hands-on sessions and live demonstrations provide more immediate feedback for new users. Provide documentation for all basic procedures, such as how to print documents on the new shared printer. Provide keyboard templates as appropriate. And establish procedures to authorize users for new levels of program access.

Practice is essential to retain any newly learned skill, so ensure that abundant opportunities are provided. Some employees are slow to adapt to change and new technology, and skillful manipulation is sometimes necessary. It is really important to consult and include employees in the planning process so that there are few surprises when a LAN is implemented and employees can see that their needs are being met by the new technology.

Another training possibility is the wide array of network courses offered commercially by consultants, training companies, users' groups, and network vendors. One thing to look for is an offering of an array of courses covering several levels of instruction related to the student's expertise with a particular system. Experience counts with network instruction. Be sure that the instructor has direct knowledge of your system and is worth an investment of your training funds. (See the chapter "Ground Zero: Training Staff," for more information.)

Summary

This chapter has been a brief overview of a very large and highly technical topic. Consult the reading list or visit the computer section of a large bookstore or library for in-depth technical information.

Planning for future network development is very difficult. The time between computer generations has diminished from 3 years to 18 months and continues to drop. Computing speeds and performance double every 18 months. Hardware and software can become obsolete seemingly overnight.

Information professionals will need to be flexible and willing to change in this volatile computing environment. Networking is one way to take advantage of technology and extend our reach. Networking can help us improve productivity for both ourselves and our users.

READING LIST

Derrick, Dan. *Network Know-How: Concepts, Cards & Cables.* New York: Osborn McGraw-Hill, 1992.

Freedman, Alan. *The Computer Glossary*, 6th ed. New York: AMACOM, 1993.

Hancock, Bill. *Network Concepts and Architectures.* Wellesley, MA: QED Information Sciences, 1989.

Howden, Norman. *Local Area Networking for the Small Library: A How-To-Do-It Manual for Librarians.* New York: Neal-Schuman, 1992.

Pilgrim, Aubrey. *Build Your Own LAN and Save a Bundle.* New York: Windcrest/ McGraw-Hill, 1992.

Schatt, Stan. *Understanding Local Area Networks*, 3d ed. Carmel, IN: Sams, 1992.

Spohn, Darren L. *Data Network Design.* New York: McGraw-Hill, 1993. For information on Datapro and Faulkner publications, contact the companies directly: Datapro (1-800-DATAPRO); Faulkner (1-800-843-0460)

TRADE MAGAZINES

Data Communications (McGraw-Hill, 0363-6399).

LAN Computing (Professional Press, 1055-1808).

LAN, the Network Solutions Magazine (Miller Freeman, 0898-0012).

LAN Technology (M&T Publications, 1042-4695).

LAN Times (McGraw-Hill, 1040-5917).

Network Computing (CMP Publications, 1046-4468).

Network World (Network World, 0887-7661)

Networking Glossary

by William Kopplin and Molly White

Discussions on computers and networks always seem to be full of buzzwords, acronyms, trademarks, jargon, and words that were thought up only five minutes ago. For example, what do you make of this bit of overheard conversion: "IPC is possible in the Windows environment thanks to Microsoft's DDE." Or how about: "PowerOpen is an ABI derived from IBM's AIX and includes the X Window System and the OSF/Motif with an optional MAS . . ." Well? Where else but in the world of computer chitchat are you going to hear mention of an OOPS (object-oriented programming system), two kinds of MAUs, two NOSes, and a "gooey" (GUI)?

This glossary is not intended to replace a current computer dictionary (if you don't already have a couple of good ones in your library--get them!); instead it is designed to help you get started on identifying and understanding some of the key networking terms so that salespeople, network programmers, systems analysts, and other techies don't go completely over your head in conversation. Mind you, in reading about LANs we found several instances of one publication directly contradicting another on a particular point. So be sure to double-check all claims against reliable sources and compare notes with other users who have had direct experiences.

If you've come across a term you can't find below, it may well be a measurement of some kind (bps — bits per second), a language (EPS — Encapsulated PostScript), a file format (GIF — Graphic Interchange Format), a category (RISC — Reduced Instruction Set Computer), a descriptive term (SVGA — Super Video Graphics Array), a very technical item (ISDN — Integrated Services Digital Network), a proprietary item (SNA — IBM's Systems Network Architecture), a specification (LU 6.2-IBM's APPC for SNA networks), or just something silly (SQUID—Superconducting QUantum Interference Device). Enjoy!

Our Definitions

Adapter: Any device that allows one piece of equipment to connect to and work with another. There is a wide variety of types of LAN adapters, and adapters are used for other purposes as well.

ADB: The Apple Desktop Bus is a standard, often-used communications port for connecting keyboards, mice, etc., to Macintosh computers.

AppleShare: Apple's software that converts a Macintosh into a file server.

AppleTalk: A baseband network from Apple using LocalTalk equipment. AppleTalk is OSI-based and uses a bus topology operating through shielded twisted-pair cable with CSMA/CD. The AppleTalk protocol and LocalTalk access are built into Macintosh computers, so no additional network interface card (NIC) is needed.

Architecture: In either computer architecture or network architecture, the word architecture refers to the total design of the system; the system itself. It includes the hardware, software, interfaces, access and control methods, bus structures, and all applicable standards and protocols.

ARCnet: This brand of network operating software, the Attached Resource Computer Network, was invented in 1977 by Datapoint; today it is supported by a variety of vendors who have developed it into a de facto industry standard. ARCnet can use twisted-pair, coaxial, or fiber-optic cable; star or bus topologies; 2.5 Mbps or 20 Mbps speeds; and a token bus protocol that forms a logical ring network. ARCnet supports a wide range of network operating systems and is a proven, low-cost solution.

ASCII: American Standard Code for Information Interchange. ASCII (pronounced ASK-key) is the most generic data coding format. Sometimes erroneously used synonymously with DOS, but not to be confused with DOS. ASCII files have no special escape codes or other unusual characteristics that are added to files by word processing or other programs. When files are converted to ASCII format, any special characters are stripped off, and thus some formatting or other information may be lost.

ATM: Asynchronous Transfer Mode is an advanced specification for very fast, high-performance networks. It involves a packet-switching technique that experts believe will eventually supplant Ethernet, token ring, and possibly even FDDI to become the networking standard of the future. ATM offers scalable bandwidth and thus is an excellent candidate for graphics-intensive transmissions. ATM is suitable for both LANs and WANs and is fast becoming the method of choice for connecting different types of networks together.

AUTOEXEC.BAT: An AUTOmatic EXECute BATch file is a special DOS batch file that always runs when the computer is first started. The AUTOEXEC.BAT file tells the computer what other programs, such as application programs or menu systems, need to be started.

Background: In the world of multitasking, the task you don't watch being executed on the screen is "background," while the task you do watch is usually referred to as "foreground." Network processing typically goes on in the background.

Bandwidth: A measurement of how much information a communications line, transmission channel, or network cable can carry. It is usually expressed in hertz, or cycles per second. The wider the better; that is, the more bandwidth that is available, the more information that can be transmitted.

Batch file: A file containing a number of DOS commands. The intent is for the commands to be executed one after the other, just as if you had typed them in. Useful when command sequences need to be repeated. The AUTOEXEC.BAT file is a good example of a batch file. Users can create their own batch files, if necessary.

Binary file: A file containing data or commands in a computer-readable format. A binary file cannot be read either through the DOS "TYPE" command or by opening a word processing package. Compare with *text file*.

Boot, booting, or booting up: Loading the computer's operating system into the computer's memory. This is what happens when you turn the computer on (a cold boot) or reset an operating computer, typically with the CONTROL-ALT-DELETE keys (a warm boot).

Bridge: A common interconnection between two networks that are both using the same communications method, identical address structures, and the same kind of transmission medium. Bridges function at the lower level of the OSI model and thus may not be capable of transmitting all messages between networks. Also refers to the equipment necessary to make such an interconnection.

Buffer: A temporary storage device that conveniently handles data that has arrived too quickly and is waiting for processing. Commonly used in connection with the storage of output to a printer, but also used in many other situations.

Bus: In the context of networking, a bus is a simple, linear-shaped LAN topology. *Bus* is also the word that describes one of the most important components inside the computer. The computer's data bus is the data channel or pathway along which signals are sent to the other various components such as the hard drive, the keyboard, etc. Thus a network bus layout and a computer's bus are two different things functioning along the same logical lines either as the connector between workstations or as the connector between components. An extension of the computer's main data bus is known as the expansion bus (see below).

Cards: Printed circuit boards are shaped like cards, so they are sometimes referred to as cards. Cards are pieces of equipment that can be added to computers to increase their capabilities or functions. Cards go in the slots or attachment points in a computer's expansion bus. There are memory cards, coprocessor cards, and for our purposes, network cards, which are known as NICs or network adapters.

CD-ROM: Compact Disk Read Only Memory is a proven data storage mechanism using the same kind of optical disks used in audio CD players. CD-ROM disks can easily hold over 500 megabytes of information, making them ideal for storing large data files, such as encyclopedias or indexes. Changes or updates to the data can be made only through the issuance of a new disk.

Clock speed: The internal operating speed of a computer. The higher the number, the more powerful the computer. In other words, a 486 microprocessor running at 33 MHz is more desirable than one running at 25 MHz. For LAN applications and file server duties, you want the computer with the most powerful, i.e., fastest clock speed you can afford.

Coaxial cable: High-capacity communications cable, also known as co-ax. An insulated wire is surrounded by a solid shield wrapped in an external cover. There are several different types of coaxial cable, including TV, baseband, and broadband. If you have cable TV at home, it probably arrives at your house via co-ax cable. All co-ax cable provides a higher bandwidth than twisted-pair cable.

COMMAND.COM: A special DOS file that handles such tasks as displaying the prompt, interpreting and executing commands, and other chores.

Compatibility: The ease with which data can be transferred from one piece of equipment to another or from one software program to another. Incompatible equipment cannot be networked.

CONFIG.SYS: A special DOS file that takes care of loading programs such as device drivers. Changing your computer system or network setup or adding any type of peripheral equipment almost always requires changes to the CONFIG.SYS file.

Configuration: The arrangement of a computer system as defined by the details of its various units. Configuration refers to hardware, software, or both.

CSMA/CD: Carrier Sense Multiple Access with Collision Detection is a computer network communications access method that keeps messages sent through the network intact and not mixed up with each other. If two computers on a network try to send a message at exactly the same time, they "sense" the impending collision of messages and both computers stop trying to send a message. Both computers wait a random amount of time before they try again.

DB-9, DB-15, DB-25, DB-37, etc.: A very common designation for the plugs and sockets used to connect communications cables. The DB standard comes from the EIA (Electronic Industries Association). The DB refers to the physical structure of the connector. The number refers to the number of pins. Thus a DB-25P indicates a male plug with 25 pins while a DB-25S indicates a female socket with 25 pins. The plugs and sockets and their attached cables can be used for a variety of purposes, including serial or parallel interfaces, and are commonly used in making RS-232 connections. They can connect printers, monitors, and other equipment to computers or to networks.

DOS, MS-DOS, PC-DOS: The industry-standard, single-user operating system of IBM compatible computers. Originally developed by Microsoft, now commonly being supplemented by Windows and other competitors.

Driver, Device Driver: A required file used by a program to send commands to peripherals such as printers or monitors. The driver contains the precise commands and instructions needed to interact with and operate the equipment. For example, the driver knows the exact number of pixels of screen resolution a particular monitor needs. Most basic drivers come automatically with your operating system. If you add a CD-ROM, you will need a new driver.

Environment: The whole arrangement of a computer system, including the hardware architecture, the systems software (which includes the operating system and other software such as data communications and database programs, etc.), and sometimes even the programming language. In order to work, applications must meet the standards of the environment.

Ethernet: Standard Ethernet, sometimes called thick Ethernet, uses thick co-ax cable. Over a thousand workstations can be connected in a normal setup with distances between workstations ranging up to 1600 feet. Additional distance can be obtained through the use of repeaters. Thick co-ax cable is, unfortunately, resistant to sharp bends, a limiting factor in some situations. Thin Ethernet, sometimes referred to as ThinNet or CheaperNet, uses less expensive, thinner co-ax cable, which is more easily bent around curves. Distances are less, though, usually restricted to 600 feet or less unless repeaters are used. Ethernet is also available via twisted-pair and fiber-optic cables. See the discussion of Ethernet in the chapter on LAN cabling.

Expansion bus: An extension of a computer's data bus that contains a number of slots, or receptacles for various types of adapter boards. Installing an adapter board (sometimes referred to as a card) in a computer usually increases the computer's capabilities in some way, such as expanding the memory or powering additional peripheral equipment such as a modem or a CD-ROM. Network adapter boards, known as NICs, are almost always installed in the expansion buses of networked computers. Well-known buses include the ISA, EISA, NuBus, and MicroChannel. Attached equipment, including networking equipment, conforms to the standards established by the cards.

FDDI: Fiber Distributed Data Interface, the American National Standards Institute (ANSI) LAN data transmission standard specified for use with fiber-optic cable. It allows for operating speeds of up to 100 Mbps, which is significantly higher than speeds achieved with copper-based cables.

Fiber-optic: Sometimes referred to as optic-fiber or optical fiber cable, this is one of the three major types of LAN cable. The medium is made up of very small strands of glass. Each strand is a path for a beam of light that is the actual signal carrier. Also used in telephone networks. Fiber-optic cable is capable of carrying both a wide variety of signals and a large number of signals.

Foreground: In the world of multitasking, the task you watch being executed on the screen is generally considered to be "foreground," while a task you don't see is "background."

486: Short for 80486, i486, or 486DX. The 80486 in all of its many varieties is currently Intel's (the manufacturer) most popular microprocessor (the computer's brain). This "chip" comes in a variety of capabilities and clock speeds and is part of a family of microprocessors that includes the 8088 (found in the original IBM PC), the 80286, the 80386, and the new Pentium.

It competes with the family of chips (the 68030, the 68040, etc.) from Motorola that power the Macintosh line of computers. Both families are now competing with the new RISC chips, but that's another story.

GAN: Global Area Network; in the ever increasing scale of LAN, MAN, and WAN, a GAN is unlimited as far as distances are concerned. It provides truly global connections.

Gateway: A device that connects two dissimilar LANs or connects a LAN with some other computer resource like a WAN or a mainframe. Gateways are "smart" in that they have their own processors and memory and they can perform bandwidth conversions and protocol conversions. Though slower than bridges and routers, gateways are often used in large organizations with complex networks requiring interconnections between different architectures.

GIGO: Garbage in, garbage out.

GUI: Graphical User Interface (pronounced "gooey") is a graphics-based user interface that usually incorporates advanced features like pull-down menus, scroll bars, dialog boxes, and icons. Windows and OS/2's Presentation Manager are two examples of operating systems that incorportate a GUI. GUIs are alternatives to older, character-based interfaces like DOS's where all commands are typed in.

Handshaking: Signals transmitted back and forth between the nodes of a computer network that establish valid connections. Hardware handshaking, done via a dedicated control wire, is used for such things as serially connected printers. Software handshaking, usually done over greater distances, involves the use of special signals.

Heterogeneous network: A LAN that includes equipment from a variety of manufacturers. Early LANs sometimes required the equipment to be "all DOS," but today Macintoshes and other systems can almost always be integrated into networks.

Hub: The center of a star topology network or the center of a cabling system. Normally, the outlying nodes connect through the hub, not with each other. "Smart" hubs have software-based port switching that eliminates the physical rewiring of the hub's wiring closet.

Interface: Any of the logical and electrical connections between computer equipment. Commonly a serial interface or a parallel interface where a plug is attached to the backside of a computer. Synonymous with "port."

Interoperability: The ability of equipment from different vendors to exchange data with each other and still act upon that data independently. Interoperability is not possible without strict adherence to industry standards.

I/O: input/output; what you (or something) give to the computer and what it gives back to you. It may be print, it may be a screen display, etc.

ISO: The International Standards Organization, obviously, sets international standards, including the OSI model (which see). The group coordinates the activities of national standards agencies such as the American National Standards Institute (ANSI).

LAN: Local Area Network, a network that spans a limited distance, usually only a couple of miles or less. Oftentimes, LANs are limited to one building; typically used to connect a suite of offices.

LAN-aware program: A special version of an application program that functions in an network environment. Network versions of software, such as database programs, are capable of creating and maintaining shared files. Single-user versions are likely to fail when placed under the demands of multiple users, and such a situation is almost always in violation of copyright licensing.

LAN Manager: A LAN operating system from Microsoft. LAN Manager requires IBM's OS/2 operating system and uses the NetBIOS protocol. It is specifically designed for client-server networking. It is noted for its security, auditing, and optional internetworking features. It is closely related to IBM's LAN Server and 3Com's 3+ Open.

LANtastic: A peer-to-peer network operating system from Artisoft. It is popular due to its low cost and easy of use. It supports Ethernet as well as other adapters.

LocalTalk: Cables and associated connectors from Apple used to connect Macintosh computers together into AppleTalk LANs (which see).

Macro: A stored list of program commands that, when retrieved, replays the commands. A very convenient way of greatly reducing the number of keystrokes needed to accomplish a task. Macros typically automate frequently-repeated tasks such as backing up a file.

MAN: Metropolitan Area Network, a network that spans a large physical complex, many times a campus or small geographic area. Distances spanned are usually less than 30 miles. Typically, a MAN will involve a backbone network utilizing broadband technology connected with fiber-optic cabling.

MAU, MSAU: A Multi-station Access Unit is the central hub in a token-ring LAN. The MAU is the wiring unit that actually connects the workstations to the network. The acronym can also refer to a Medium Attachment Unit, which is a different piece of equipment used for Ethernet connections. There are also two NAUs, but you will have to look those up for yourself.

Multitasking: Executing more than one program at the same time on the same computer. Requires a relatively powerful computer running a relatively sophisticated operating system that directs the computer as it divides up the tasks.

NetBIOS: Network Basic Input/Output System is a system program included in recent versions of DOS. NetBIOS is the DOS standard transport protocol for linking workstations together in LANs. Application programs use NetBIOS in both client/ server and peer-to-peer models. The NetBIOS protocol matches part of the OSI model.

NetWare: The market-leading family of network operating systems from Novell. NetWare works with a wide variety of computers and networking equipment, including Ethernet. NetWare 2.x is widely used for medium-sized LANs (up to 100 users). NetWare 386 (NetWare 3.x) works with more powerful computers on larger networks (up to 4,000 computers). And NetWare Lite is designed for smaller, peer-to-peer networks (as small as two computers).

NIC: Network Interface Card, or network adapter. The NIC is a circuit card or board that must be placed in the expansion bus of each workstation in all of the most popular LAN operating systems. The NIC is an internal piece of computer equipment that must be added in much the same manner as other expansion boards, by opening up your computer or taking the back off and carefully attaching it to the right slot.

Node: A connection point in a network. *Node* is sometimes used synonymously with computer or workstation, but it can also refer to peripheral equipment such as shared printers or specialized equipment such repeaters, file servers, etc. Any junction point in a network that can create and/or receive signals.

NOS: Network Operating System, the software that controls how the network works. Comparable to the computer's operating system (such as DOS or Windows), which controls the computer, the NOS integrates the pieces of networked hardware. A computer cannot work without an operating system, and a network cannot work without a NOS. The NOS program typically contains a large group of functions and features, such as security controls, an administration interface, backup capabilities, menus, remote log-in, etc. The most crucial part is the management of the connection(s) between the server(s) and the workstations. The NOS typically forms a shell around or above the computer's operating system, intercepting appropriate commands and processing them. The best-known current NOS is Novell's NetWare, though NOS was also used as a brandname for a while by Control Data for its Cyber computers.

Novell: The company that makes the most popular brand of network software, NetWare. So predominant is Novell that you sometimes hear the phrase "a Novell network" even though there are all kinds of Novell networks.

OSI model: The Open System Interconnection is a model that serves as the foundation for efficient communication among different networks and within a network. The model has seven layers of specifications. Happily, more and more vendors are supporting the OSI standard.

Packet switching: An advanced technique for controlling a high volume of transmission traffic in a large network.

Parallel interface: A multiline port, or channel, used for transferring data in multiple simultaneous pieces. Printers attached to computers via parallel interfaces are often connected with standard Centronics (originally a brandname, now a type) 36-pin connectors. Eight wires are commonly used at the same time for data transfer (the other wires are used for various control functions).

Peripherals: Auxiliary equipment attached by cables, usually, to the central computer. Some examples of peripherals are printers, external disk drives, numerical keypads, trackballs, external modems, CD-ROM drives, scanners, etc.

PhoneNet: Network products from Farallon that can extend the distances over which AppleTalk-LocalTalk networks can be operated. PhoneNet uses ordinary unshielded twisted-pair phone cable.

Platform: The architecture or characteristics of a particular computer (Macintosh, for example) or family of computers (IBM-compatible, for example). It is the standard to which programmers write their software. The operating system is often included in discussions of platforms, although programming languages are not. (See *Environment.*)

Plug-compatible: A peripheral that requires no modification to the interface in order to be fully connected to another manufacturer's equipment and operational is said to be plug-compatible. When the device is plugged in, it should be ready to function.

Port: Ports are interfaces between the computer and the outside world (other pieces of equipment usually). External ports are sockets or plugs, usually found at the back of the computer, for connecting equipment through the use of various kinds of cables. Most computers have several different kinds of ports, usually both serial and parallel varieties, for different kinds of communication tasks. Internal ports are expansion bus sockets that accept controller cards for devices like disk drives and monitors.

Protocol: A defined, standard means of data communications such as the early TTY, or teletypewriter protocol. Protocols determine the signals and the processing of those signals. There are many different kinds of protocols and dozens of examples of each kind. Some common LAN protocols are Xerox's XNS/ITP (Xerox Network Systems/Internet TransPort) and Novell's IPX (Internet Packet EXchange) and SPX (Sequenced Packet EXchange). There are too many more to even attempt to list them all.

Repeater: A device that simply amplifies or regenerates a data signal in order to send the signal over longer distances.

Router: A common interconnection between two dissimilar, physically distinct networks. Routers act as a store-and-forward message relay system. Routers contain a common network address that is known to all attached networks. Because of the complexity involved, transmission times for messages sent across routers may be slowed considerably.

RS-232-C: A well-known EIA (Electronic Industries Association) standard for a serial interface. Can be used with either a 25-pin or 9-pin connector. Normally restricted to transmitting data over just a few feet, with the right kind of high-quality cable, transmission distances can be increased to several hundred feet.

RS-422: The first in a series of EIA standards for extending serial communications across greater distances than that allowed by RS-232. Often uses a 37-pin connector.

SAN: The Storage Access Network, from Vinca, is a specialized LAN that features advanced techniques for handling data storage devices like hard drives; in essence, a hard drive server.

SCSI: Small Computer System Interface (pronounced "scuzzy"), an industry-standard interface for connecting peripherals to computers. It features an 8-bit bus interface. Macintosh computers, with their built-in SCSI ports, have fueled the popularity of this connection method.

Serial interface: A port, or channel, used for input/output that transfers data in a serial fashion, one piece after the other. Serial connections are often used for communications; thus modems are often connected to a computer's serial port. Mice and scanners are also frequently connected this way. See RS-232-C.

Sex changer, gender changer: A special cable connector, or coupler, that reverses the gender of one of the cable ends, or plugs, so that two female connectors or two male connectors can be joined together.

Shell: Just as a seashell surrounds a sea creature, a software shell is a special program that fits around or above the main program. You get to the program, sometimes without your knowledge, by going through the shell. Shells are typically add-on programs that give a menu-driven front end or graphical user interface to a program or operating system in order to improve the interface and make the program easier to use. There are quite a few commercially available shells for UNIX and DOS, as well as for other programs and networking systems. The latest versions of DOS now come with a a built-in shell.

Slots: The receptacles for cards. Slots are internal computer attachment points where printed circuit boards of all types, including network interface cards (NICs), are attached to the computer's expansion bus.

SMTP: Simple Mail Transfer Protocol is a very common E-mail protocol used in TCP/IP networks.

SneakerNet: Transferring files between users through the use of their tennis shoes. Sometimes referred to as NikeNet.

Spool, Spooling: Simultaneous Peripheral Operation On Line. When multiple files are sent to the same printer, the files are spooled, that is, stored and queued in the printer buffer until each can be printed in turn. A peripheral storage device may be used for the buffer. The advantage to spooling is that once the buffer has the file, the originating computer is free to pursue some other task.

Standards: Recommended or required methods of data communication and networking. The major international agencies publishing such documents are ANSI, CCITT, EIA, IEEE, and ISO. Each agency is responsible for creating and promoting hundreds of standards. Some vendors are so successful that their products have become de facto industry standards, witness the Hayes-compatible modems. Evaluate carefully any claims about standards, for in the world of computers standards are many times no more than negotiations between manufacturers.

STARLAN: A well-known network from AT&T that uses a star or bus topology. Twisted-pair, coaxial, or fiber-optic cable can all be used. STARLAN networks are baseband products consistent with the OSI model using CSMA/CD.

Superserver: A powerful computer with a larger-than-normal amount of memory and disk capacity, acting as a network server. Superservers often use multiple processors and provide high-speed multiprocessing.

TAN: never mind.

TCP/IP: Transmission Control Protocol/Internet Protocol. Originally developed by DARPA in the 1970s, it is now a very widely used and supported industry standard for communication between networks.

10-Base[X]: Several IEEE committees developed widely used standards for LAN topologies. The standards specify access methods and are all based on the OSI model. The most important ones are from the 802.3 subcommittee on the CSMA/CD bus standard, the 802.4 token bus standard, the 802.5 token ring standard, and the 802.6 metropolitan area network standard (MAN). These are often referred to by their nicknames, such as

10Base5, which refers to a bus network with thick baseband coaxial cabling that transmits data at 10Mbps over a 500-meter maximum distance. There are several of these well-known standards for Ethernet networks.

Text file: A file of straight ASCII characters with no extra control, command, format, or escape characters. Text files can be displayed with either the DOS "TYPE" command or through the use of a commercial word processing program.

Topology: The way in which LANs are designed, arranged, and wired. How the pieces of equipment are connected together and how they communicate with each other. There are two types; centralized, such as a star topology, and decentralized, such as a bus or ring topology.

Twisted pair: Two, thin-diameter (22 to 26 gauge) insulated wires commonly used in telephone wiring. The wires are twisted around each other to minimize interference. If the wires were straight, they would pick up unwanted signals much like an antenna. Sometimes abbreviated as UTP, or unshielded twisted pair, although twisted pair is available both with and without shielding.

UNIX: A multiuser, multitasking operating system originally developed by Ken Thompson and Dennis Ritchie at AT&T's Bell Laboratories in the early 1970s. UNIX's long development and maturation have cummulated in System V Release 4.0, which was originally released in 1989. UNIX (pronounced "yoo-nicks") is really a group of programs driven by cryptic commands (for example, in DOS you "rename" a file; in UNIX you "mv" a file) that have recently been helped by the introduction of easier-to-use shells, such as NeXTStep, Open Look, and OSF/ Motif. UNIX is written in a highly portable language, C, and can be used by many types of computers, from mainframes to micros. The word UNIX comes from a single-user (UN) version of MULTICS, an earlier operating system, even though UNIX's greatest inherent strengths are connected to its built-in multiuser capabilities.

UPS: An Uninterruptible Power Supply can supply backup power to computers whenever the main power supply fails. When a UPS is interconnected with a network file server, all network users can be alerted to save their files in the event of a power failure. UPSs often contain surge protectors, battery backups, voltage regulators, and other filters that help ensure that the network receives clean reliable electric power.

User interface: The combination of screen design, menus, icons, mouse input, commands, on-line help, etc., which together dictate how easily a user can interact with a computer. Well-designed user interfaces can sell computers, witness the Macintosh.

VAN: A Value Added Network is usually a commercial entity that provides additional services beyond simple data transmission, such as data storage and forwarding. Telnet is a well-known example.

Vaporware: Software that people talk about but that doesn't actually exist, yet.

VINES: VIrtual NEtworking System is a UNIX-based network operating system from Banyan Systems that operates on a wide variety of computer equipment. Its strengths are security, flexible and varied connections, and its ability to be customized with a multitude of options.

WAN: A Wide Area Network spans such distances that major connections involve dedicated telecommunications circuits equivalent to long-distance telephone circuits. A WAN frequently provides national connectivity.

Workstation: A computer that serves a single user as opposed to the file server, which serves all users on the network. Usually, but not always, implies a high-performance computer capable of specialized tasks such as scientific or graphics applications. May refer to the group of computer equipment typically found on a desk or simply to any terminal or personal computer.

Jo Anne Newyear
Life Science/Undergraduate Librarian
The General Libraries
The University of Texas at Austin
LLJN@utxdp.dp.utexas.edu

5. CASTING THE INTERNET

For any information professional, the Internet presents a challenge to be conquered or at least managed effectively. Representing a vast ocean of information possibilities, it has begun to change the standards of how library facilities operate and conduct information-gathering routines. It will never be the only source we rely on for information needs, but eventually it will be regarded as a medium with which information professionals will be required to have a relevant degree of competency.

Because the Internet is new, rapidly changing, and unfamiliar, many information professionals are at a loss on how to tackle this monster. The best advice, repeated over and over again, is to first utilize this resource for your own professional development. This approach build on your interests and background in the materials related to your profession and therefore engages your patience, tenacity, and curiosity to explore.

The tips and information in this chapter are introductory; they should lead you to a better understanding of where to find the real information you need, or at least how you and your information center may successfully approach the challenge of the Internet.

Some History

Most people first ask, "What is the Internet anyway?" The Internet is a "superhighway" of many interconnected computer networks mainly in North America but extending worldwide. These networks operate under the Transmission Control Protocol/Internet Protocol (TCP/IP) with the major backbone of this supernetwork provided by National Science Foundation's NSFNet. In simpler terms, the Internet is a network of networks that have agreed to share pipelines of access that send messages in bulk from point to point for distribution to individuals or other networks. Generally, the Internet was developed for users who are engaged in research or educational tasks.

Three major functions are supported by the Internet:

1. SMTP or Simple Mail Transfer Protocol
2. Telnet or remote log-in
3. FTP or File Transfer Protocol.

With all these acronyms flying around you may wonder what TCP/IP is. It is the foundation that the Internet is built upon--a software package that allows dissimilar computers to communicate. In other words, it allows your computer to talk to other computers without your having to worry about the how and why.

Hierarchically arranged, the Internet keeps local traffic local while Internet traffic is routed through gateways. The National Science Foundation network, which is funded by government grants, provides and supports the major high-speed links between the regional and local networks. Originally designed to connect supercomputers, the Internet has undergone explosive growth in the past five years. As a result, plans have been developed to set up a National Research and Education Network (NREN) to provide and support more growth and more interconnectivitity between networks at higher rates of speed than the 9600 baud rate.

The Internet, as we call it today, was originally started in 1969 under the name ARPANET (Advanced Research Projects Agency Network). This project, funded by the Defense Department, was decommissioned in 1990. The ARPANET was originally conceived to aid researchers in sharing information and resources. The use of the Internet continues today as a nonprofit avenue for research collaboration. From its original inception it has evolved into a valuable information, communication, and educational resource. At present the National Science Foundation oversees most of the administration of the network.

Some readers may be aware of the major initiative underway that will greatly enhance the Internet and transform it into NREN (National Research and Education Network). The legislation to enact NREN was introduced by Vice-President Albert Gore while he was a senator from Tennessee. It was recently passed in the U.S. Congress, becoming the High Performance Computing Act of 1991. To all of us end users, this means that the Internet will develop more of an educational framework opened up to colleges, universities, schools at all levels, and the general public, providing greater interconnectivity between various systems, information sharing, and enhanced communication at higher speeds. Essentially, we are moving toward the creation of the "virtual Library"; no one will be information poor.

The Coalition for Networked Information, CAUSE, the Association of Research Libraries, and Educom are all working to help promote NREN and the development of networked information resources. They hope to build a comprehensive directory to all textual information available through the Internet. This is now underway, and a directory is available that lists electronic journals, newsletters, scholarly discussion lists, and interest groups. This directory is available from the Association of Research Libraries for $10 to members and $20 to nonmembers. Many of the Internet guides you can purchase include mini directories of good sites to search and pointers to archives.

Currently, there is no central support facility to assist users of the Internet. Any support that is available is through the regional networks or through individual institutions. Most of the guides that are available about the Internet give listings of all the regional networks and provide detailed support in the terms of tips, instructions, and referral listings. Your best bet is to buy a good general Internet guide and keep it by your keyboard.

So What's the Big Deal?

OK, so the Internet sounds somewhat interesting, but why should special libraries be interested in all this heady computer network stuff? For starters, any information professional who has to keep abreast of current trends, self-development activities, and issues may find that this pursuit of self-development can affect their worktime. Professional self-development usually entails extensive travel time, research, reading of professional literature, attending conferences and workshops, and making professional contacts. Not to mention your inevitable financial investment to participate in these endeavors. For obvious reasons, librarians in isolated areas or who manage one-person operations are at a great disadvantage when it comes to the cultivation of professional development.

Without leaving the library you have to find a way to stay on top of developments in your area of information expertise. That's where the Internet can help. You don't need travel — you can connect to remote sites to determine library holdings or develop your own collection, talk to a colleague, particpate in collaborative efforts, read full-text journals, "publish," search the literature, participate in conferences, search databases, access OPACs, download state-of-the-art shareware and other software, or even scan help-wanted ads for a better job. The Internet has so much to offer information specialists, it's difficult to believe it's only in the infant stages of its evolution.

The following items are just a taste of what you may find of interest "out there" in the Internet.

ON-LINE LIBRARY CATALOGS

Connecting to large on-line public-access catalogs, or OPACs, such as one of the hundreds of available universities, can help with bibliographic and collection development functions, cataloging, interlibrary loans, and electronic delivery of documents or files.

ELECTRONIC MAIL / CONFERENCE COMMUNITIES

Probably one of the most common uses of the Internet is communication between colleagues. One form of this is through computer conferences, discussion lists, or newsgroups. There are also bulletin boards and usenet groups. A survey of special librarians who are Internet users indicated that they used E-mail extensively for many reasons, from communicating with colleagues to servicing interlibrary loan requests. The new Ariel Service offered by the Research Libraries Group provides delivery of scanned documents over the Internet.

ARCHIVES OF SOFTWARE

In archives across the Internet, there is more software than you can imagine available to you for free or at very low cost. Most of this software is freeware or shareware. Large archives of Macintosh software exist at Stanford via anonymous FTP to host sumex-aim.stanford.edu.

DATABASES OF SPECIALIZED INFORMATION; PERIODICAL INDEXES

Many information specialists will have a keen interest in the number of databases available over the Internet. Many OPACs contain databases from molecular biology to patents, campuswide information systems, bulletin board systems, and wide area information service (WAIS).

ELECTRONIC JOURNALS, REFERENCE BOOKS

A number of publishers and societies are beginning to provide full-text journals such as the Online Journal of Current Clinical Trials and The Scientist via the Internet.   In addition, many sites have reference materials such as Roget's Thesaurus, the Oxford Book of Quotations, the CIA Factbook, and complete texts of the Bible, the Book of Mormon, and Shakespeare's plays. The full text of many public-domain works, such as Alice in Wonderland, The Wizard of Oz, and Moby Dick, are also available through Project Gutenberg (to obtain copies anonymous FTP to host mrcnext.cso.uiuc.edu; login anonymous; cd etext). (See the chapters "Building Your Electronic Reference Base" and "Am I Ready for Electronic Journals?" for more information.)

COMMERCIAL SERVICES

Many commercial on-line systems, including Dialog (telnet dialog.com), BRS (telnet brs.com), Mead (telnet 192.73.216.21), and OCLC, STN (telnet stnc.cas.org), can now be accessed over the Internet. The Internet assumes the telecommunication functions and can be much less expensive and much faster than the traditional telecommunication services .

MONEY-SAVING OPPORTUNITIES

Internet users pay lower telecommunication fees — potentially much lower if your computer department picks up most or all of the charges. For example, Dialog charges about $12 an hour connect time through commercial services (Sprintnet, CompuServe, Tymnet, Dialnet). The Internet charges about $3 per connect hour. If time is money, then think about the fact that the Internet operates at a baud rate of 9600 and above.

With the librarian's focus on providing more services for less money in economically constraining times, the Internet is a resource that can help. However, you will need to have the attitude of a facilitator of information. Maybe your clients already use the Internet. Can you improve upon what they already know? Take stock of what the Internet can do for you as a station for information gathering, information delivery, and marketing your library's services. Think about: giving demonstrations of unique finds; actively exploring the Internet so you can find sites to answer questions you are often asked; assisting clients who may not know as much as you do about the Internet — they will love you for it; locating topical discussion groups for your clients or yourself—this serves also to advertise your organization as a "player"; developing handouts to intoduce the various service points of the Internet (see the end of this chapter for sample handouts developed for subject-oriented clientele).

How Do You Get Hooked Up?

The first step is to see if your organization is on a computer network and if there is a connection to the Internet. Many people have access to the Internet and just don't know it. There are several ways to do this: ask someone who may know, or look up your organization in a reference tool that lists networks. As a general rule all academic libraries should be able to access the Internet. Many research institutes, government agencies, and large corporations probably are connected too. Check out the public library; some offer a service called Freenet — a community-based information and E-mail system allowing Internet access. You may have to check with these sources to see if you can get an account with access. No matter who you are, you should be able to get access to the Internet through a service provider. Needless to say, providers will offer varying degrees of service at varying ranges of cost. You need to decide which features you need and comparison shop.

DEDICATED INTERNET ACCESS

Large institutions that want Internet access should examine getting dedicated access because this will give them all the stops and whistles — complete access to the Internet for computers in that institution. This will involve the addition of some communications hardware, which can be expensive, but once installed it is a very flexible connection that allows every computer in that facility to have full network functions. Given this type of investment, dedicated Internet access is most suitable for a large group of users.

DIAL-UP ACCESS / SERVICE PROVIDERS

If you can't afford dedicated access, just sign on with someone who already has dedicated access. Basically, you would be dialing up a computer that is connected, allowing you access through its gateway onto the Internet. Since you are sharing this access with others, the cost may be greatly reduced; however, some service providers charge per-hour access fees on top of your monthly dues. The upside of this option is that you probably already have all the hardware and software you will need. The downside is that you will be able to do only what the service provider allows you to do. Usually this means that you are given a gateway to the Internet but only in the form of electronic mail exchange. Beware of access to limited services. In addition, you may also have to pay the long-distance charges unless you are given a local access number. Service providers represent a very competive market. Check with the National Science Foundation Network Service Center for a current list of network providers.

INTERNET SOFTWARE

Several versions of Internet software are available that run over normal phone lines using at least a 9600 baud modem. One example is SLIP (Serial Line Internet Protocol), a software package that is used to run Internet Protocol (IP) over telephone lines. It will let you run Telnet, FTP, and other services from your local modem-equipped workstation.

You are never very far from an Internet connection. Local universities are an obvious link, as are local library consortia. Recently a standard service provider called CLASS (Cooperative Library Authority for Systems and Services) announced a plan that is open to any library in the country: join CLASS for $135 a year — getting all its other benefits — and pay an additional $150 a year for a single-password account to the Internet ($50 for each additional password) plus $4.50 per connect hour. The CLASS connection is a full-featured Internet connection-access to telecommunications (telnet), File transfer (FTP), and bulletin boards. Call 800-488-4559 for more information. Just keep in mind that some service providers give connections that allow only E-mail or telnet, or will send messages only one way.

Cost is probably going to be the major factor in any decision you make, but buyer beware — examine fully what you get, or you may end up getting shortchanged. Things to consider:

- How well does the provider give user support and training if at all?
- Is the pricing fair and accurate in light of the services and access you will be receiving?
- Will the cost deter you from using the service?
- Is it easy to use?
- Does it offer a full range of services such as E-mail, Telnet, FTP, and Finger?

Once you have an account you will need to learn how to use the software to access the Internet. This is of the more difficult aspects of the Internet challenge. Frequently, help is available on-line, but if you can't get on-line, what do you do? Once again, a good reference guide to Internet applications will be invaluable to you . Keep in mind that many professional organizations and universities are offering skill-building courses for the Internet.

Another tool that may make Internet access easier for you are the specialized software packages developed for certain operating systems that serve as menu-driven gateways to remote systems on the Internet. These menu-based packages are very useful because they identify sites and initiate the connections for you. An example is the LIBS software written for the DEC VAX VMS or the UNIX operating system. Mark Resmer of Sonoma State University developed this menu-driven gateway. If you would like to try it out, TELNET to vax.sonoma.edu or 130.157.2.3 and log-in as "LIBS."

Another location that has slightly adapted the LIBS software is the University of Texas. Its menu system is called UTINFO and is based on Mark Resmer's LIBS software; to connect, TELNET to utinfo.cc.utexas.edu, at the username prompt enter "utinfo" and then follow the directions on the screen.

HYTELNET is another software package developed to assist users in reaching all the Internet-accessible libraries, Freenets, and campus-wide information services via Telnet. Designed for IBM-compatible or Unix-based computers. HYTELNET was created by Peter Scott of the University of Saskatchewan (scott@sklib.usak.ca).

A few other applications you may want to look into are NCSA Telnet software, XferIt, Hyper FTP, X-Library and Turbo Gopher. The NCSA Telnet software exists for both the PC and the Macintosh and is available via anonymous FTP from host ftp.ncsa.uivc.edu. If you need the PC version, go to directory NCSA Telnet, subdirectory PC/Telnet, filename telxxbin.zip. The xx stands for the version number. The Macintosh version is the Mac/Telnet subdirectory, filename telnet.x.sithqx. XferIt is a Macintosh application that will enable you to transfer files to and from computers using an easy, consistent interface while recognizing a variety of transfer modes and FTP servers. To obtain a copy of this shareware, contact Steven Falkenburg (sfalken@apple.com). HyperFTP is another FTP client stack very similiar to XferIt, but it is not able to transfer material from the same variety of other hosts. For more information about HyperFTP, contact Douglass Hornig (DUG@cornellC.CIT.Cornell.edu). X-Library is a library-oriented communications program for the Macintosh that allows connection to a variety of remote services, including multiple services being active at any one time. This program requires a Macintosh with a Communications toolbox and Hypercard 2.0 or later. This shareware product is available for anonymous FTP from host ftp.ucsc.edu, directory Mac/comm or host sumex-aim.stanford.edu, directory Info-mac/comms. TurboGopher is an application that lets you search archive sites at maximum speeds and is available for anonymous FTP from boombox.micro.umn.edu in the /pub/gopher/Macintosh-TurboGopher directory, or contact gopher@boombox.micro.umn.edu for more information.

If you do succeed in transferring these software packages, remember that the files may need to be decompressed. For information on retrieving software over the Internet, consult a good general guide that will walk you through the do's and don'ts of software transfer.

Now You Are Hooked Up, What Can You Do?

The first step is to join a few choice discussion groups that pertain to libraries. This will enable you to become familiar with current issues and people who might be important contacts, not to mention enabling you to build your skills in manipulating mail protocol functions. E-mail (where you communicate with, most likely, one person) is a little different from another unique form of communication available on the Internet — discussion lists or conferences. These conferences or discussions are managed by listservs. The listservs are large mailing lists that serve to distribute electronic group discussions covering a broad array of subjects, including libraries. In order to subscribe you must communicate with the listserv. One of the biggest listservs of interest to librarians is PACS-L (Public Access Systems in Libraries). Other library listservs deal with various topics, including Reference(Libref-L), Bibliographic Instruction (BI-L), Cataloging (Autocat), and Interlibrary Loan (ILL-L).

To subscribe to one of these you usually send a message to the list's listserv and say SUBSCRIBE list name your name. You will then receive a message confirming the subscription and various instructions particular to the list. These might include how to submit comments, etiquette, the moderator's E-mail address, etc. The moderator is the person or group of people responsible for maintaining the list and the content of the discussions.

Most of the new Internet guidebooks have excellent chapters that describe not only the types of lists you can subscribe to but also how to do it and include troubleshooting tips. I would recommend Ed Krol's book for any beginner (see under General Guides in the Recommended Reading section at the end of this chapter.)

Once you feel comfortable exchanging mail and somewhat at ease with the Internet medium, you are probably ready to try Telnet. By using Telnet you can log-in to remote sites and access that site's resources, whether databases or OPACs. Remote log-in is basically a resource-sharing service. It allows a user to connect to any machine on the Internet and conduct business as if directly attached to the remote system. Most often this can be done from anonymous users, but some locations may require accounts. The range of machines on the Internet is vast and each type has its own particular settings and parameters, but Telnet takes care of this for you. You need not worry about settings, baud rates, parity bits, or flow control, as you do with most standard communications programs. Telnet sets up a virtual terminal interface in which all the details are handled for communication.

To connect is simple enough: run Telnet and supply the address of the remote system. Usually an address appears as a set of letters or numbers. To locate the addresses of various sites, consult one of the many Internet guides (see Recommended Reading). Once a connection is established to the remote site, you will probably use commands and select services that may be unfamiliar to you. So be patient. Some points to consider in light of the extensive variety of computers being used is that sometimes the keys are different. Occasionally, communications programs translate terminal keys to the personal keyboard but sometimes not. The type of terminal emulation usually used by Telnet is DEC VT-100. But when connected to an IBM 370-type computer, a 3270 emulation is used. Consequently, the function keys may not respond as they usually do. Some server programs require a connection to a port, and the method of doing this can differ in different versions of Telnet. Some OPACs assume that you are using a directly connected terminal and provide no way to exit. So what can you do? Try ALT-X or CTRL-Q or F10. Check to see what version of Telnet you are using and make note of your escape keys in advance.

FTP — The Final Frontier

Usually, the third step in Internet skill building is FTP, which many people find a much harder task to master.

FTP provides for transfer, over the network, of ASCII text or binary data from a host computer to a local computer at your site. Many Internet documents and software are available through FTP. Many FTP sites have huge directories of text files and software that a user can download, or copy. You can also upload, or send, files to other systems. You may assume that to have access to material like this you would be required to have a password, but the convention of distributing this material via anonymous FTP makes it relatively easy to transfer files to your machine. The process essentially allows the user, by creating an FTP connection, to log-in to the host site as an anonymous user using an arbitrary password, such as the word "guest" or the user's E-mail address. Once inside the system you can move around in directories and locate files of interest that you would like to transfer to your computer or account.

Many FTP archives are mounted on UNIX computers. Knowledge of basic UNIX files, FTP commands, and the ability to interpret UNIX directory listings may help you. When you log-in to a host FTP site, assume that it may be case-sensitive and enter directory and file names as they appear. Directory names are usually pretty descriptive, but when in doubt start with a directory called pub. Sometimes sites offer an INDEX file to assist users in identifying the file they need. Almost all the guides and books recommend that when FTPing, you get the readme and index files first. These files may tell you about the resources that are available at that site. Take advantage of Network Information Centers (NICs). These sites are set up to provide users with all sorts of information about the Internet and its resources. These NICs usually contain good navigating documents. (Try these: NIC.DDN.MIL; NISC.SRI.COM; NIS.NSF.NET; and PIT-MANAGER.MIT.EDU.)

SAMPLE ANONYMOUS FTP SESSION

FTP	Open connection to FTP site on
Internet	Log-in as anonymous
Username: anonymous	Password: guest Type in guest or your E-mail address
DIR	Directory command
CD pub	change directory to pub
Get ftp.list	Get file called ftp.list (before you get the file may need to set the type of transfer)
Quit	Close the connection

Be aware that this example is a simple one for retrieving a text file. If you are trying to retrieve software or images or some other nontext file, you will need to change the transfer format. Check with your computer consultant, colleague, or handy Internet reference for advice. Transferring software and images can be tricky. They may be compressed, which means that you will need the appropriate software to decompress them. Don't be discouraged — it is a trial-and-error process in the truest sense. Just remember to be tenacious: if you have trouble, check the directory you're in, try the "ls" command to list all the files in the current directory; if the file is not there, move up a directory using "cdup", then change to the appropriate subdirectory with "cd directory name".

Another way to find the file you need is to use Archie. This is a service that can be used for subject access to FTP archives — it will search for words or root words associated with the subject you type in. It is an electronic database of all the files contained within almost every anonymous FTP site on the Internet in the world. The fastest Archie server is: archie.ans.net. (147.225.1.2). Log-in as "archie" — no password is required.

Is There a Map to This Place, or How Do I Get There From Here?

Before you begin an Internet session, decide what format and subject you are interested in. Do you want software, images, or text? Your particular need or interest will determine where to go and where to look.

Navigation tools are the best way of finding pointers to possible sites or files that you may want. Representative examples of such tools are WAIS (wide area information server), Gopher, and World Wide Web. As the Internet grows and expands, users are recognizing the need to utilize navigation tools to identify resources. Due to the absence of an overall directory or index to the Internet, librarians must cope with the need to know what's out there and how to get it. Although there is no way for someone to know everything that's out there, librarians need to develop the necessary navigation skills to wade through the Internet.

Gopher is an application providing access to Internet resources using an interface that in effect burrows through the Internet, linking up with OPACs and campuswide information systems and allowing you to browse and search documents. Items of interest can be mailed to your E-mail address. Some choices through Gopher will actually connect you to remote sites or servers. What Gopher does for you appears seamless, so you may not know exactly where you are, what you are doing, or how you got there. A much faster way to cruise Gopherspace is the new Gopher client TurboGopher. Contact gopher@boombox.micro.umn.edu for more information about this new utility. Veronica (Very Easy Rodent-Oriented Netwide Index to Computerized Archives) is a service that maintains an index of titles of Gopher items and provides keyword searches of those titles. Access to Veronica is submitted via a Gopher client, which will in effect search the menus of hundreds of Gopher servers to locate your keyword input. For more information, contact Fred Barrie (barrie@futique.scs.unr.edu) or Steven Foster foster@veronica.scs.unr.edu). Jughead is a another Gopher tool that has been recently developed to assist users with Gopherspace. This tool differs from Veronica in that it searches files of just one Gopher. For more information, contact Rhett Jones (jonzy@cc.utah.edu).

How to connect? Telnet to gopher.micro.umn.edu

Go to the directory named Other gopher and information servers. Select that item and search titles in Gopherspace using Veronica.

WAIS, or Wide Area Information Server, is a program that assists searching through the Internet for documents that contain the search word(s) you select. Thus you can retrieve information from many different databases on the Internet through a common interface. You begin by selecting from a list of sources the ones that most likely contain the information you are seeking. These sources are actually servers on the Internet that can contain repositories of text files, software, images, or access to on-line catalogs and databases. After selecting the sources to be searched, you then type in your keywords describing your subject. WAIS then connects to the sources you have selected and presents you with a ranked list of documents of likely interest. For more information, contact George H. Brett (george.brett@cndir.org).

How to connect? Telnet quake.think.com (192.31.181.1)

Log-on as WAIS; user ID your user name, Term vt100 will get message starting swais.

World Wide Web (WWW) is a program that utilizes hypertext to let you browse rapidly through information sources on the Internet. Basically, links are established between documents so that you can move from one document to another. Documents may be text files, which can be displayed, or indexes, which can be searched. You have the option of returning home or to the original screen you began with. The project leader is Tim Berners-Lee (timbl@info.cern.ch) at CERN, the European Physics Laboratory in Geneva, Switzerland.

How to connect? Telnet info.cern.ch (128.141.201.74)

Netfind is a tool that provides Internet users with a "white pages" to the Internet. When given the name of a user and a description of where the user works, the tool attempts to locate the telephone number and E-mail address of the person sought. For more information, contact jam@ccu.nersc.gov.

How to connect? telnet bruno.cs.colorado.edu

login netfind

Whosis is a program that will respond with information about a person similar to white pages. It is maintained by DDN Network Information Center. There are many Whosis servers on the Internet. Check out an Internet Guide for more details or contact mhpower@athena.mit.edu. A list of Whosis servers is available via anonymous FTP from host sipb.mit.edu, directory pub, subdirectory whosis, filename whosis-servers.list.

Finger is a Unix-based tool that lets you examine the user log file on a system. This allows you to find out someone's log-in name or perhaps full name. You would need to know what computer the person uses and his or her name or ID. Check a guide for more information.

Mark Kantrowitz (mkant@cs.cmu.edu) of Carnegie-Mellon University has produced a comprehensive list of techniques and sources for locating people's E-mail addressess. You can contact him or get the document via anonymous FTP to host a.gp.cs.cmu.edu, several directories in cd/afs/cs.cmu.edu/user/mkant/public/email, filename college-email.text.

This is a small sampling of the navigation tools out there for you to use. Remember that all these navigation tools are still under development and are themselves rapidly changing. To utilize these tools will take time; they are evolving, as is the Internet, on a daily basis. Using these tools in a timely and efficient manner to deliver information is an ongoing challenge.

Training the Staff

Probably the most difficult aspect of the Internet information world is the problem of how we train our staff or instruct our users to utilize this new resource. This new superhighway of interconnected networks will be viewed as an information resource, and people will turn to the information professional for assistance in navigating the Internet. Recently, much focus has been given to the standardization of interconnectivity among systems for the development of network environments, but this concept should also be applied to our approach in training library personnel. The library support staff is often overlooked, and yet they are usually the ones who handle the bulk of our frontline questions. This should be seen as a way for the library or information center to be an agent of change, progress, and innovation. It is important to nurture exploration and training, but you will need to monitor their effect on work flow and productivity. Once a certain point is reached someone must assess whether the Internet is a reliable and useful information resource.

Try to be the first unit in your organization to gather information about the Internet, and encourage your staff to explore and discover utilities that would be of interest to your library and your clientele. Once you develop novice expertise, think about developing tailor-made handouts or documentation that will better serve your clients. (See the sample handout at the end of this chapter.) Maybe you will gather together a list of appropriate discussion lists or Telnet sites. You might create a current awareness service from information in discussion lists, bulletin boards, and electronic journals. Locate free or shareware software for your library or clients. Think hard about how the Internet can enable you to develop new services for your clients. Take a lead in training your staff to utilize these resources — your unit will stand out.

Remember that gathering information, developing professional contacts, and building expertise are ongoing processes. You will need to allow time each day for you and your staff to explore. This may seem a lot to ask, but think about the possible return. This could be an excellent way to market your information center and make use of a number of potentially costly information providers for little or no cost. The Internet places at your disposal a medium for the exchange of ideas, discussion of relevant problems, and solutions to problems. No longer will you feel isolated. You will become a part of a much larger community and reap the benefits of such an arrangement.

RECOMMENDED READING

General Guides

ALA Reference and Adult Services Division (RASD). *Library Resources on the Internet: Strategies for Selection and Use.* Available via anonymous FTP from dla.ucop.edu; directory pub/Internet; filename libcat-guide.

Internet Resource Guide. National Science Foundation Network Service Center. Available via anonymous FTP from host nnsc.nsf.net, directory resource-guide.

Kehoe, Brendan P. *Zen and the Art of the Internet: A Beginner's Guide to the Internet, 2d ed.* Prentice-Hall, 1993. ($22.00)

Kochmer, Jonathon. *The Internet Passport: NorthWestNet's Guide to Our World Online, 4th ed.* NorthWest Net. 1993. ($39.95)

Krol, Ed. *The Whole Internet User's Guide & Catalog.* O'Reilly & Associates, 1992. ($24.95) This is a must buy, one of the best guides that includes the how's, the why's, and the where to go's.

Laquey, Tracy L. *The User's Directory of Computer Networks* Bedford, MA: Digital Press, 1990.

Laquey, Tracy L. and J. C. Ryer. *The Internet Companion: A Beginner's Guide to Global Networking.* Addison-Wesley, 1992. ($10.95)

Malkin, Gary. *FYI on Questions and Answers: Answers to Commonly Asked "New Internet User" Questions. Network Working Group, Request for Comments 1325.* February 1991. Available via anonymous FTP from host ftp.nisc.sri.com, directory rfc, filename rfc1325.txt.

Polly, Jean, "Surfing the Internet: An Introduction," *Wilson Library Bulletin*, 66 (10) (June 1992): 38-42.

Quarterman, J. *Recent Internet Books*. RFC 1432 (March 1993). Available via anonymous FTP from host ftp.nisc.sri.com, directory rfc filename rfc1432.txt.

Tennant, Roy and John Ober and Anne G. Lipow. *Crossing the Internet Threshold: An Instructional Handbook*. Library Solutions Press, 1993. ($45.00) Another good one; very concise and understandable instructions, not too technical and great tips and tricks.

The entire issue of the September 1991 issue of *Scientific American* was devoted to the Internet — check it out.

Library Catalogs and Telnet Addresses

St. George, Art and Ron Larsen. *Internet-Accessible Library Catalogs and Databases*. Available via anonymous FTP from host ariel.unm.edu, directory library, filename Internet.library.

Raeder, Aggi and Karen Andrew. "Searching Library Catalogs on the Internet: A survey." *Database Searcher*, Sept. 1990, pp. 16-31.

Barron, Billy. *Accessing On-Line Bibliographic Databases*. Available via anonymous FTP from vaxb.acs.unt.edu directory Libraries.

Libsoft archive has documents via through FTP from host hydra.vwo.ca on WAIS, CWIS, Archie, Bulletin Boards

FTP Information

FTP Sites List. Available via anonymous FTP from host pilot.njin.net; directorypub; filename fto-list.

Listserv Information and Electronic Discussion Groups

A complete listing is available from Charles Bailey Jr. University Libraries, University of Houston, Houston, TX 77204-2091; BITNET: LIB3@UHUPVM1.

Charles Bailey's "Library oriented Computer conferences and electronic serials on Bitnet and Internet. *Database Searcher*, Feb.-March 1991, pp.22-23.

Interest Groups. Network Information Systems Center. Available via anonymous FTP from host ftp.nisc.sri.com. directory netinfo, filename interest-groups.

Sites of listserv — listserv@ubvm.bitnet list global

Usenet Information

Quartermain, John. S. *The Matrix: Computer Networks and Conference Systems Worldwide.* Bedford, MA: Digital Press, 1990.

Rapaport, Mathew. *Computer Mediated Communications: Bulletin Boards, Computer Conferencing, Electronic Mail, and Information Retrieval.* New York: Wiley, 1991.

Mail Guides

Chew, John. *The Inter-Network Mail Guide.* Available via anonymous FTP from many sites including hosts.

Frey, Donnalyn and Rick Adams.!%@::*A Directory of Electronic Mail Addressing and Networks*. O'Reilly & Associates. 1991. ($26.95)

Internetwork-mail-guide. Available via anonymous FTP from host ftp.msstate.edu — directory ftp/pub/docs/, filename Internetwork-mail-guide.

New York guide. Available via anonymous FTP from host ariel.unm.edu — directory ftp/library, filename newyork.guide.

Document Delivery

Contact Ariel Coordinator, RLG, 1200 Villa St., Mountain View, CA 94041-1100; 415-691-2284; bl.msr@rlg.bitnet.

Electronic Journals and Books

Strangelove, Michael and Diane Kovacs. *Directory of Electronic Journals, Newsletters, and Academic Discussion Lists.* Association of Research Libraries, 1992. Also available via anonymous FTP from host ksuvxa.kent.edu directory library; filename Acadlist. Or contact Diane Kovacs (dkovacs@kentvm.kent.edu).

Project Gutenberg is led by Michael S. Hart (hart@vmd.cso.uiuc.edu); for information about what electronic books are available, conduct anonymous FTP to host mrcnext.cso.uiuc.edu (128.174.201.12), directory /etext and its subdirectories.

On-line Access

Notess, Greg R. "Gaining Access to the Internet," *Online*, Sept. 1992, pp.27-34.

Information about SLIP- FTP to host ftp.nisc.sri.com, locate RFC 1055.

SLIP software available from host nic.cerf.net in var/spool/ftp/pub/ slip directory.

LIBS software — contact Mark Resmer (mark.Resmer@sonoma.edu) available via anonymous FTP to sonoma.edu, directory/pub, filename libs for VAX VMS version or libs.sh for the Unix.

WAIS software — FTP to host think.com, directory wais or contact Barabara Lincoln (barbara@think.com), project leader for WAIS.

List of Regional Networks and Service Providers — National Science Foundation Network Service Center. Network Provider Referral List. Available via anonymous FTP from host nnsc.nsf.net, directory nsfnet, filename referral-list.

Special Libraries

Tillman, Hope N. and Sharyn T. Ladner. "Special Librarians and the Internet," Special Libraries, Spring 1992, pp.127-131.

SAMPLE HANDOUT 1 - BITNET AND LISTSERVS

USING BITNET FOR ELECTRONIC DISCUSSION LISTS AND CONFERENCES

I. WHAT IS AN ADDRESS?

The Internet address: jqpublic@ibmpc.biology.washington.edu

contains the following parts:

jqpublic .... a "user-id" (User Identification)
@ .... "this user-id is located at"
ibmpc .... a particular Internet host within
biology .... the biology department at the University of Washington Campus
Network within
washington .... the Internet in Washington State, within
edu .... the education-oriented portion of the Internet in the U.S.

The Internet guide on how to send mail to anyone on the Internet with an explanation of all the different possible mail addressing schemes. is compiled by John Chew and is called the Inter-Network Mail Guide. It is available via anonymous FTP from many sites including:

ariel.unm.edu -- in the directory ftp/library/newyork.guide
ftp.msstate.edu -- in the directory ftp/pub/docs/ Internetwork-mail-guide
pitt-manager-mit.edu -- in the directory pub/usenet/comp.mail.misc/Inter-network_mail_Guide

or send the message GET NETWORK GUIDE to LISTSERV@UNMVM.bitnet

II. WHAT IS BITNET?

Bitnet (Because It's Time Network) is a general purpose academic network chartered to facilitate noncommercial information exchange among its members. Founded originally to link CUNY with Yale, it has grown to over 500 American college and universities, plus colleges and universities in Canada (known as NetNorth), Europe (EARN), Latin America, Australia, Africa and the Far East.. An Internet/ Bitnet connection exists through many gateways in many places. Properly addressed mail should have no problem being interchanged between the two. To receive an electronic users guide to BITNET send a GET BITNET USERHELP message or command to NETSERV@BITNIC.

III. LISTSERV DISCUSSION LISTS

LISTSERV is a computer program installed on a computer in the BITNET network which manages "discussion groups" or "lists" for people who have shared interests.

LISTSERV discussion lists are topic-oriented forums distributed by e-mail, dealing with a wide variety of topics. Once you've subscribed to a LISTSERV discussion list, messages from other subscribers are automatically sent to your electronic mailbox.

LISTSERV discussion groups make it easy for you to communicate with other people about a particular topic, without having to know their user-ids or e-mail addresses ahead of time.

SAMPLE HANDOUT 1 - BITNET AND LISTSERVS

The LISTSERV service is like an electronic newspaper, except every "article" is sent to you seperately. Subscribing to a LISTSERV discussion group is also similar to subscribing to a newspaper, except that you and a Listserver communicate with e-mail, instead of postal mail. You find out what lists are available and request subscription or cancellation by sending e-mail to a Listserver. A listserver uses e-mail to handle subscription information and to distribute messages to and from subscribers.

To subscribe, unsubscribe, or perform other functions involving communicating with the LISTSERV program, you send mail to the LISTSERV at a particular node on the bitnet.

IV. HOW TO SUBSCRIBE TO A LIST:

Once you know the name of a list and the node id of a list, send a message in the form:

subscribe listname your name your institution

to the listserv at the appropriate node id.

For example, to subscribe to the Biomedical Ethics discussion, send the message

subscribe biomedical ethics Jonathan Hart UT at Austin

where "Jonathan Hart" would be your name and biomedical ethics is the name of the list you want to subscribe to. Send this message to the address:

LISTSERV@NDSUVM1

Note that the subscription request is sent to "listserv", not to the list name, and that you use your actual name in the message, not an E-Mail name or identifier.

Users of the IBM VM computer can use the TELL command to make requests to the LISTSERV application directly, as follows:

tell listserv at node id subscribe listname yourname

For example, to subscribe to the Computers in Biotechnology list:

tell listserv at hdetud1 subscribe ebcbbul Melville Dewey

POSTING MESSAGES: Once you have subscribed, you can post messages to a list by sending an E-Mail message addressed to the list name:

listname@nodeid.BITNET

For example to post a message to the Artificial Neural Networks list, you would use the address:

neural-n@andescol.BITNET

LISTSERV will send back a notification when your message was successfully distributed.

SAMPLE HANDOUT 1 - BITNET AND LISTSERVS

ARCHIVES: The messages sent to a list are saved each month in a log file, which you can retrieve by sending an E-MAIL message in the form:

get listname logyymm

to the address

listserv@nodeid.BITNET

yymm is the year and month for the period you want.

DEFINITIONS:

Listserver or listserv- A listserver is a special kind of user account; instead of a person at the other end of am electronic address there is software that maintains distribution lists, stores files and responds to your commands.

Listname- the 1-8 character by which a distribution list is identified to the listserver. Originally most listnames ended with -L (ethics-L) but less common now.

List@node- the electronic address of the list the address to which mail and files must be sent in order to be distributed to the list. It is the listname plus the listserver node (EISSIG@ASUACAD)

Listserver@node- the electronic address of the listserver--the address you use to join or resign a list get help etc. (LISTSERV@ASUACAD for all commands)

NOTE: Whereas you send mail to be distributed to a list@node commands are sent to listserver@node. Be careful not to confuse the two; occasionally a user requests help from a "list@node" and everyone receives the request.

Brief List of Basic Listserv Commands Commands are listed with the minimum acceptable abbreviation in capital letters. Angle brackets < > are used to indicate optional parameters		
SUBscribe	listname<full_name>	Subscribe to a list, or change your name if already subscribed
SIGNOFF	Remove yourself:listname	From the specified list
SET	Mail/NOMail	Toggle receipt of list mail
CONFIRM	listname1<listname2<...>>	Confirm your subscription (when LISTSERV requests it)
GET	filename	Obtain a file from a list, obtain record of previous messages on list
INDex	listname	Sends a directory of available archive files for the list, if postings are archived
Lists	Global	All known lists, one line per list, sent as a (large!) file
Informational commands		
Help		Obtain a list of commands
Info	<topic>	Order a LISTSERV manual, or get a list of available ones (if no topic was specified)

SAMPLE HANDOUT 1 - BITNET AND LISTSERVS

IV. FOR MORE INFORMATION ABOUT THE INTERNET AND DISCUSSION LISTS:

1. For a file showing the names and node ids of LISTSERV lists, by sending the exact message

   list global

to the address:

   listserv@bitnic

2. Here are the names and titles of some RFCs and FYIs considered to be of general interest to Internet users. Where applicable, both the FYI and the RFC number are given, but using the FYI number will always assure the reader of getting the latest version of the document.

nis.nsf.net in directory /Internet/publications/rfc
ftp.nisc.sri.com in directory /rfc and /fyi
uu.psi.net in directory /rfc.

RFC 1118The Hitchhiker's Guide to the Internet
FYI 3, RFC 1175FYI on Where to Start: A Bibliography of Internetworking Information.
FYI 4, RFC 1206Answers to Commonly Asked "New Internet User" Questions
FYI 7, RFC 1207Answers to Commonly Asked "Experienced Internet User" Questions
RFC 1208Networking Glossary of Terms
FYI 10, RFC 1290There's Gold in Them Thar Networks!

3. There is a "list-of-lists" file available on the host ftp.nisc.sri.com that lists most of the major mailing lists, describes their primary topics, and explains how to subscribe to them. The file is available for anonymous ftp in the netinfo directory as interest-groups (that is, the path is netinfo/interest-groups). It can also be obtained via electronic mail. Send a message to mail-server@nisc.sri.com with the body of the message reading, "Send netinfo/interest-groups" and the file will be returned in moderate size pieces via electronic mail.

4. The Directories of Academic E-Mail Conferences

The Directories of Academic E-Mail Conferences contains descriptions of 800 electronic conferences on topics of interest to scholars. The directory entries are split up by category based upon the dominant academic subject. Topic descriptions are taken in whole or part from the descriptions provided by each listowner, editor, moderator or coordinator to the New-List, the List of Lists, and the Internet Interest Groups file.

SAMPLE HANDOUT 1 - BITNET AND LISTSERVS

Access

Anonymous FTP to ftp ksuvxa.kent.edu, directory LIBRARY. The file ACADLIST.README provides an introduction guide to the directory.

Contact

Diane K. Kovacs - One of the Moderators of LIBREF-L
Instructor, Reference Librarian for the Humanities
Kent State University Libraries
Kent, Ohio 44242
Phone: (216) 672-3045
E-mail:DKOVACS@kentvm.kent.edu

5. This section lists information about the Internet and places you might retrieve information on discussion groups and conferences. This material was organized by John December (decemj@rpi.edu).

INTERNET DESCRIPTIONS	ANONYMOUS FTP	HOST FILE OR DIRECTORY
Hitchhikers Guide	ftp.nisc.sri.com	rfc/rfc1118.txt
Gold in Them Thar Networks!	ftp.nisc.sri.com	rfc/rfc1290.txt
Zen & Art of Internet	ftp.cs.widener.edu	pub/zen/
Guide Internet/Bitnet	hydra.uwo.ca	libsoft/guide1.txt
NSF Resource Guide	nnsc.nsf.net	resource-guide/
CERFNet Guide	nic.cerf.net	cerfnet/cerfnet_guide/
Internet Monthly Report	nis.nsf.net	Internet/newsletters/

DIRECTORIES	ANONYMOUS FTP	HOST FILE OR DIRECTORY
Internet Resource Dir	ftp.virginia.edu	public_access/*.txt
Interest Groups List	ftp.nisc.sri.com	netinfo/interest-groups
Library Access Script	sonoma.edu	pub/libs.sh
Electronic Conferences	ksuvxa.kent.edu	library/acadlist.readme

SAMPLE HANDOUT 2 - BITNET AND LISTSERVS

USING TELNET

I. WHAT IS TELNET?

TELNET is basically an interactive communications program that allows you to remotely log on to other systems to access all kinds of services and resources ranging from campus wide information systems, library catalogs, full-text databases, and bulletin board systems. It is the standard TCP/IP (Transmission Control Protocol/Internet Protocol) remote log-in protocol. The term "TELNET" refers to the remote login that's possible on the Internet because of the TELNET Protocol. The use of this term as a verb, as in "telnet to a host" means to establish a connection across the Internet from one host to another. Usually, you must have an account on the remote host to be able to login to it once you've made a connection. However, some hosts provide public services that do not require a personal account.

II. HOW DO I GET STARTED?

In order to access TELNET, you would need to have a dedicated terminal on a local network or dial up access to the local network which has a gateway to the Internet node. Try contacting a department computing liaison person to get access or the Computation Center on campus.

III. HOW TO CONNECT USING TELNET?

If TELNET is installed on your computer, you can usually type "telnet", followed by another computer's Internet address. An address could be in the form as a name as the one below or in can take the form of a numeric address. Sometimes you will also have to type in a user id or other login information.

For example, to login to the University of Maryland's INFO program, you'd type:

telnet info.umd.edu

If your system responds then it may say "connecting". It should be successful by stating it has connected to that address. If nothing else happens you may press <CR> to let the remote system know you are there. However, the computer in Maryland will prompt you for a login id; so just type "info" after the words "To Log On:"

To Log On: info

You will then be asked what kind of terminal you are using. To take full advantage of this particular TELNET site, you should type "vt100," or some other full screen emulation terminal type which allows you to use cursor keys, etc. Throughout this session, you will see instructions on your screen about what to do. If you get confused in this or any other TELNET session, just type "help" or "?". Or, go to the section entitled "TELNET Troubleshooting" for solutions to some of the more commonly encountered problems. Here's a list of a few of the many Science TELNET sites on the Internet which offer valuable and interesting services. Enjoy!

SAMPLE HANDOUT 2 - BITNET AND LISTSERVS

IV. TRY SOME OF THESE SELECTED SCIENCE SITES:

American Math Society BBS

To Connect: telnet 130.44.1.100
To Log On: e-math
Password: e-math

This database includes an author index to mathematical reviews of over 93 topics including astrophysics, biology and other sciences. Also includes electronic distribution of Bulletin of AMS.

Environmental Protection Agency National Catalog

To Connect: telnet epaibm.rtpnc.epa.gov
First Menu select PUBLIC ACCESS
Second Menu select OLS

Consists of several databases including citations and summaries for items cataloged by the 28 EPA libraries and EPA reports distributed through NTIS and the hazardous waste collection.

Food and Federal Drug Administration

To Connect: telnet 150.148.8.48
To Log On: bbs

Register as requested, you'll find reports and press releases on FDA. To get on-line users manual type manual at the prompt and hit enter. Then type 1.

Lunar and Planetary Institute (NASA)

To Connect: Telnet LPI.JSC.NASA.GOV or 146.154.14.11
To Log On: Username: type lpi
To Log Off: select exit and logout from main menu

Select information services from main menu; provides information resources on geology, geophysics, astronomy and astrophysics.

PennInfo

TO Connect: Telnet penninfo.upenn.edu or 128.91.254.116
To Log Off: type Q

Massive collection of information on the university, libraries computing resources, electronic texts, and MEDINFO database.

South East Florida AIDS Information Network

To Connect: Telnet callcat.med.miami.edu or 129.171.78.1
To Log On: library

Select L on main menu; Select 1 on next menu.

STIS Science and Technology Information System

To Connect: telnet stis.nsf.gov or 128.150.195.40
To Log On: Public

Supernet International (HPCwire): the Free Online News and Information Service for High Computing

To Connect: telnet hpcwire.ans.net or 147.225.1.51
To Log On: hpcwire

SAMPLE HANDOUT 2 - BITNET AND LISTSERVS

You will need to register as a user but this is a free service. Very easy to use interactive menu system which features include daily news on high performance computing, trade show, job bank, research register, loads of Internet information and guides.

UTINFO

To Connect: telnet utxvms.cc.utexas.edu
Username prompt: utinfo
Follow the directions on screenon how to use this system. This system allows you to access a variety of online library catalogs, databases and resources including subject areas in the sciences.

Weather information

To Connect: telnet hermes.merit.edu or 35.1.48.150
To Log On: type um-weather at the which host? prompt

V. TELNET TROUBLE-SHOOTING

Step 1. If just typing "telnet" doesn't give you the TELNET> prompt, try typing "help telnet", "man teln et", or "info telnet" or whatever command is appropriate to your operating system. You might also try "tcpip" instead of "telnet" or contact your local user services personnel.

Step 2. If you type "telnet Internet computer address" and you don't get connected "unknown host" message, you might have misspelled the computer's domain name, or the domain name of the computer might have changed.

"foreign host did not respond within OPEN timeout" message: There's probably too much traffic somewhere on the Internet between you and the host, or the host is disabled in some way. Try again later.

There might be a limit on the number of users allowed onto the host at a given time. You will usually get some sort of explanation from the host to this effect. Try again later.

SAMPLE HANDOUT 2 - BITNET AND LISTSERVS

Step 3. When logging into a VM/CMS mainframe from a UNIX host, TELNET will only give you "line-at-a-time" service. You should use a 3270 emulator for full screen service.

VI. FOR MORE INFORMATION ON TELNET AND THE INTERNET

Adams, Rick and Frey, Donnalyn: !%@:: A Directory of Mail Addressing and Networks, 2nd Ed. Sebastopol, CA: O'Reilly & Associates, 1990.

Health sciences resources on BITNET/INTERNET
    Access: ftp.sura.net
    Directory:pub/nic
    file: medical.resources

Kehoe, Brendan P. Zen and the Art of the Internet: A Beginner's Guide. 2nd ed. Englewood Cliffs, NJ: Prentice Hall, 1992.

St.George, Art. and Larsen, Ron. Internet-accessible library catalogs and databases. Available: e-mail: LISTSERV@UNMVM.BITNET message: get library package.

Yanoff, Scott. Special Internet Connections. available at hpc.wire@hpcwire.ans.net.

The following is a list of information sites about the Internet compiled by John December (decemj@rpi.edu).

SAMPLE HANDOUT 2 - BITNET AND LISTSERVS

INTERNET DESCRIPTIONS	ANONYMOUS FTP HOST	FILE OR DIRECTORY
New User's Questions	ftp.nisc.sri.com	fyi/fyi4.txt
Hitchhikers Guide	ftp.nisc.sri.com	rfc/rfc1118.txt
Gold in Networks!	ftp.nisc.sri.com	rfc/rfc1290.txt
Zen & Art of Internet	ftp.cs.widener.edu	pub/zen/
Zen ASCII version	csn.org	pub/net/zen/
Guide Internet/Bitnet	hydra.uwo.ca	libsoft/guide1.txt
NSF Resource Guide	nnsc.nsf.net	resource-guide/
NWNet Internet Guide	ftphost.nwnet.net	nic/nwnet/user-guide/
SURANet Internet Guide	ftp.sura.net	pub/nic/infoguide.*.txt
NYSERNet Internet Guide	nysernet.org	pub/guides/Guide.*.text
CERFNet Guide	nic.cerf.net	cerfnet/cerfnet_guide/
DDN New User Guide	nic.ddn.mil	netinfo/nug.doc
AARNet Guide	aarnet.edu.au	pub/resource-guide/
Internet Monthly Report	nis.nsf.net	Internet/newsletters/
Internet Maps	ftp.merit.edu	maps/
Internet Resource Dir	ftp.virginia.edu	public_access/*.txt
Electronic Journals	ftp.eff.org	pub/journals/
Barron Library Catalogs	ftp.unt.edu	library/
St. George Lib Catalogs	nic.cerf.net	cerfnet/cerf net_info/library_catalog/
Technical Reports	daneel.rdt.monash.edu.au	pub/techreports
Online Library Catalogs	hydra.uwo.ca	libsoft/guide2.txt
Library Access Script	sonoma.edu	pub/libs.sh

SAMPLE HANDOUT 2 - BITNET AND LISTSERVS

VII. TELNET ESCAPE KEYS

When using the "libs" gateway on the UT Vax Cluster the Telnet escape key is always Control-C Q (this is what you use with the Worldwide menu on the Library Information Stations). To interrupt a Telnet session between a Macintosh and the VAX you can use APPLE-K (caution this leaves the port on the remote host up and running, for example if you were connected to Tennessee when you used this key - the Tennessee computer would keep an open port for you until it timed out, this is bad computer etiquette and you may receive charges); better to use APPLE- C to close the session or if you must, APPLE-Q to quit.

In the following chart are Telnet escape keys for different systems:

SYSTEM	PACKAGE	ESCAPE KEYS
MS-DOS	NCSA TELNET	ALT-X
MACINTOSH	NCSA	COMMAND-C (TO CLOSE SESSION)
VAX/VMS	CMU	CTRL-C
	MULTINET TELNET	CTRL-Q
	MULTINET TN3270	CTRL-C Q
UNIX	TELNET	CTRL-] Q
	TN3270	CTRL-C Q

SAMPLE HANDOUT 3 - BITNET AND LISTSERVS

Internet Resources:
Biological Sciences

Developed by Craig Schroer

The sources below represent a small sampling of the information resources pertaining to the Biological Sciences which are available on the Internet.
Many of these resources may be accessed via the General Libraries
Macintosh Information Stations.

Library Catalogs

The following library catalogs are particularly strong in humanities sources. Consult Subject Collections by Lee Ash Z/731/A78/1985 to discover the best libraries for specific subject areas such as: China-History.

Yale (telnet HOLLIS.HARVARD.EDU when connected press return, then type HOLLIS)
University of Michigan (telnet HERMES.MERIT.EDU when connected type MIRLYN)
University of California System (telnet MELVYL.UCOP.EDU)
Columbia University (telnet CAL.CC.COLUMBIA.EDU, login as CALENDAR)
Carnegie   Mellon   University   (telnet CMULIBRARY.ANDREW.CMU.EDU, login as LIBRARY)
Massachusetts Institute of Technology (telnet LIBRARY.MIT.EDU)
University of Illinois, Champaign/Urbana (telnet GARCON.CSO.UIUC.EDU, Logon: User: lcs)

General Libraries Macintosh Information Station

The following Internet resources in the biological sciences may be accessed through the Worldwide Information Menu option on any of the General Libraries Macintosh Information Stations. These databases provide such information as job postings, ongoing research projects (i.e., drosophila genome mapping), grant opportunities, biology related software, and selected journal articles. From any Information Station Main Menu use the following path
Databases of Special Interest/UTINFO/Databases and Information Services/Science.
You will see a menu which includes the databases:

MEDINFO - U. Penn Med. School -- Contains ftp site addresses for obtaining
the table of contents for journals which are posted on the BIOSCI
BIO-JOURNALS bulletin board. Also contains information on available grants, NIH grant writing, fellowship opportunities, etc.

NATIONAL SCIENCE FOUNDATION -- Provides access to information regarding grant
opportunities, job openings, technical reports, etc.

SAMPLE HANDOUT 3 - BITNET AND LISTSERVS

GENBANK - Gene Sequence Info.-- provides access to gene sequence information.

Additional Resources:

Genetics and Molecular Biology Databases:

LiMB Database--Listing of Molecular Biology Databases
Contents: A central listing of molecular biology databases, their internet
        addresses, contents, institutional affiliations and usage criterion
        (i.e. free vs. fee).
FTP Host: ncbi.nlm.nih.gov
directory: repository/LiMB
file: limb

ENZYME--Dictionary of 3072 enzymes.
Contents: information about catalytic activity, cofactors, and diseases
        associated with various enzymes. Cross references to the SWISS-
        PROT dataset.
FTP Host: ncbi.nlm.nih.gov
directory: repository/ENZYME
files: enzyme.dat and enzyme.asn

Bibliography of Theoretical Population Genetics
Contents: An extensive bibliography of journal articles about genetics
        and inheritance.
FTP Host: evolution.genetics.washington.edu
directory: bible
files: bible.ac through bible.sz

IuBIO--Indiana University Archive for Molecular and General biology
Contents: A public archive of biology data and software including
        extensive drosophila data and an archive of biology news from
        Usenet.
FTP Host: ftp.bio.indiana.edu
file: Archive.doc

Electronic Mail Conferences:

The following is a short list demonstrating the diversity of E-Mail conference groups on
biology-related topics. These conferences are an excellent source of information, and offer
a quick way to ask a question or obtain advice from a subject specialist. One way to obtain
a complete list of biology related E-Mail conference groups is to access the information
server at the University of Pennsylvania (telnet NISC2.UPENN.EDU) and then locate the
following document -- Libraries/Internet & Related Information/Internet (& other network)
Resources/Bibliographies/Scholarly Electronic Conferences [Kovacs} 5th Rev./Biological
Sciences.

SAMPLE HANDOUT 3 - BITNET AND LISTSERVS

INFO-GCG@UTORONTO
Covers topics in computer-aided molecular biology.
HUMEVO@GWUVM
Examines human biological evolution, adaptation and variation.
BNFNET-L@FINHUTC
Discussion group for biological nitrogen fixation
ETHOLOGY@FINHUTC
Discusses animal behavior and behavioral ecology.
LPN-L@BROWNVM
Laboratory Primate newsletter list
BIOMED-L@NDSUVM1
Discusses biomedical ethics
CLIMLIST@OHSTVMA
Climatology discussion list
BIOTECH@UMDD
Biotechnology Discussion List

Usenet News Groups

Like the academic listserv mail conferences listed above, Usenet newsgroups are a good way to participate in worldwide discussions in a particular subject area. Below is a truncated listing of newsgroups in the Biological Sciences.

bionet.general	bionet.molbio.ageing
bionet.molbio.genbank	bionet.population
bionet.virology	bionet.neuroscience
bionet.immunology	bionet.biology.tropical
sci.bio.technology	sci.environment
Arabidopsis_BioSci.src	IUBio-fly-clones.src

IV. THE TRUE ELECTRONIC JOURNAL — STILL A DREAM

When did users first dream about the time when "all information would be on a computer"? But a better question is, when did they begin to expect that journals would soon be on-line and free? Today's students, those people so familiar with computer games, bulletin boards, and sysops, seem to be expecting something that, while technically possible and a growing reality, is not as pervasive as users think or want. Unfortunately, no one knows the answer to the real question — and it's a big one — *who will pay?* The answer is important. If individuals are willing to pay, then libraries may be very different in the future. But if history is any predicter of the past, most users won't or can't pay. Until we know who will pay, it will be hard for libraries, publishers, and scholars to invest in true electronic tools — those that allow direct electronic access to data and information.

Even if thousands of electronic journals are some way off, we still need to know more about the capabilities of those that do exist. The following is a discussion from someone with electronic journal experience. We can all benefit from her experiences and knowledge.

Nancy Elder
Head, Life Science Library
The General Libraries
The University of Texas at Austin
LLNIE@utxdp.dp.utexas.edu

6. AM I READY FOR ELECTRONIC JOURNALS? ARE ELECTRONIC JOURNALS READY FOR ME?

Several alternative formats are currently developing for journals. This still-developing area warrants your attention, but more for its potential than for today's reality. The formats currently available and on the near horizon are full-text journals on-line from commercial database vendors; image files of journals on CD-ROM, floppy disk, or other electronic media; and true electronic journals.

Full-Text Journals On-line

Dialog, BRS, Lexis/Nexis, STN, and other commercial database vendors already have substantial files of full-text journals on-line. Among the various vendors several hundred titles are available. The preponderance of them are business and law. There is also an increasing number of science titles, especially chemistry (American Chemical Society) and medicine. *BiblioData Fulltext Sources Online* (1) is an excellent guide to full-text journals. It is arranged alphabetically, and for each journal it tells which vendors have files available, file names or numbers, and dates of coverage.

How might you use these? Currently, true electronic journals consist of text only and are not an image of the original article. This means that illustrations, tables, charts, and even the references may be omitted from the text supplied. This text can be manipulated using other software after it has been downloaded. Depending on the circumstance, your users may find this more or less appropriate. Some users may object to the un-journal-like appearance. The cost per article varies depending on the rates of the vendor and on your skill in retrieving the desired item. Most of these files can be used for subject searching or for known-item retrieval. Depending on your collection and the subject areas for which you may want to retrieve articles, you may find a large number of journals of interest or none. Coverage may start or stop at just the wrong date for your query. All these factors make this a somewhat unreliable delivery method. However, your user may think you are superlibrarian if you can download the text of the article he is desperate for and have it on his desk in 12 minutes. In a pinch, tables, charts, and appearance may not seem critical. If you already have accounts with database vendors, be sure you are familiar with their full-text files. If you don't have accounts, you should investigate to see which vendors have the most appropriate full-text files for your needs.

Image Files on CD-ROM

Complete articles available as images on CD-ROM are now available in several subject areas. The largest of these services are the ProQuest files from University Microfilms, ProQuest Social Sciences Index/Full Text, and ProQuest General Periodicals Index/Full Text. Adonis, produced by a consortium of European publishers, provides access to about 220 biomedical journals. Image files have the distinct advantage of offering both indexing and text retrieval in one package. Image files are not directly searchable and cannot be manipulated. Copies made from the commercial image files on laser printers are typically high quality. However, the ProQuest files also index articles that are not included in the image file. Approximately 40% of the articles indexed do not have images available*. The expense of Adonis (both system and per article) is sufficiently large to rule out many special libraries. Again, the issue of timeliness must be addressed. As services of this type develop, they may well offer a viable alternative for small libraries for indexing and text, if there is a service well matched to your information demand. A sample articles are included in Appendix V.

In addition to services that provide article images on CD-ROM, there is an increasing number of individual journals available on CD-ROM. Some of these are an alternative to print, some are an alternative to on-line, and for some CD-ROM is the only format. *Ulrich's 1992-93* lists 559 serials available on CD-ROM (2). However, only 107 of these are journals or newsletters. The majority are directories, indexing services, or other reference material. CD-ROM journals may be a viable alternative to microform as the number of titles available continues to increase.

---

*Images are not available for a variety of reasons, but most commonly it is because of concerns about royalty payments and that users will cancel subscriptions.

True Electronic Journals

True electronic journals are, for the most part, a dream still waiting to come true. A small number of journals are beginning to appear that are accessible on the Internet or other networks, generally for no cost or for only the cost of using the network. A few, such as *Online Journal of Current Clinical Trials*, are supported by associations in conjunction with some kind of network utility (*OJCCT*— from AAAS and OCLC). There are also a myriad of listservs on the Internet, some of which are journal-like. There are also such phenomena as the distribution of preprints of articles among research groups in physics. For the long run, or even the short run, this is primarily a developing concept. *Directory of Electronic Journals, Newsletters and Academic Discussion Lists* (3) provides a good list of Internet sources, a bibliography of network sources, and a bibliography of articles on electronic publications. There is little of immediate utility especially given the likely demands in most special libraries. This area should be watched for developments in the near future. *Directory of Electronic Journals, Newsletters and Academic Discussion Lists* identifies 240 journals and newsletters, up from 110 in 1991, and identifies 1,152 discussion lists, up from 517 in 1991. A sample of electronic journals and newsletters lists is provided in appendix. There are hundreds, or even thousands, of electronic discussion lists and interest groups. The topics tend to be specialized, the discussions may not be focused, and some discussion lists are prolific and require a substantial time commitment. A few may be worth investigating for yourself or your users.

REFERENCES

1. *FULLTEXT SOURCES ONLINE for Periodicals, Newspapers, Newsletters & Newswires.* Ruth M. Orenstein, ed. Needham Heights, MA: BiblioData, 1993.

2. *Ulrich's International Periodicals Directory* 1992-93. 31st ed. New Providence, NJ: R. R. Bowker, 1992.

3. *Directory of Electronic Journals, Newsletters and Academic Disscussion Lists*, 3d ed. Strangelove, Michael and Diane Kovacs. Washington, DC: Association of Research Libraries, 1993.

[1]Images are not available for a variety of reasons. But most commonly it is because of concerns about royalty payments and that users will cancel paper copies.

V. SPECIALIZED PROGRAMS—THE WAVE OF THE FUTURE

LANs, Internet, and other electronic information access systems will bring information right to the workstations and libraries of the world. In the past users had to guess where specific information might be found or which library might have a particular book. Part of this has been made much easier with OCLC and Internet. Now users can find out which library has a particular book. However, while they can find out, for example, which library owns *Mark's Standard Handbook of Mechanical Engineering,* they can't see if it covers coaxial cable or gives soil compaction figures for draglines.

In order to find out this level of specific information, libraries will need special access programs. We need to develop services that link, coordinate, and instruct users in the various kinds of information sources — electronic and old-fashioned — since we can't really hope that every word ever written will eventually be on some computer somewhere. Without these links users will have a hard time knowing where to look for information. Should they use Internet, a local LAN, a file loaded on a stand-alone computer, or an old print journal? How will they know what is cost-effective and the fastest? Luckily there are several interim solutions available until the time when everything is electronically accessible arrives.

One solution is to buy a menu program such as Direct Access or Saber Menu. Both are designed so that users can choose preselected options from a menu by a click of the mouse or a simple keystroke. Once an option is selected, the menu program then runs an "autoexec.bat" type of file and brings the selected file, LAN, or Internet address to the user. By using a menu, similar programs or topics can be grouped into categories — for example, "local library catalogs." Once this category is selected, the user is shown a list of local libraries within driving distance. The potential is really endless.

One library has developed an opening workstation menu that lists several specific library catalogs on the Internet by name, along with several locally relevant listservs and a list of the databases on the local CD-ROM network. The benefit to users is obvious — they don't need to know or remember dial-up instructions, passwords, IDs, and computer identifiers, because all of this is loaded into the menu.

Another benefit is that menus are very easy to use—for both the staff and the client. Staff do not need to have any programming experience; all that is needed is the computer address and password.

Menu programs provide real service to our users in this changing and complex environment. But sometimes this is not enough. Sometimes users need more in-depth help, such as detailed instruction on how to use the system or what to do with the information once it has been gathered. The next two chapters talk about two very specific ways to do this. Both can add value, manage the information glut, and generally give clients better service. These are expert systems and hypercard.

Susan B. Ardis
Head, McKinney Engineering Library
The General Libraries
The University of Texas at Austin
LLSBA@utxdp.dp.utexas.edu

7. Expert Systems

What Is an Expert System?

An expert system is a computer program that emulates the behavior and knowledge of human experts within a specific domain or area of knowledge and, as a result, performs with the proficiency of a human expert. In addition to performing on the level of an expert, an expert system:

- represents the expert's domain-specific knowledge in the same way the expert uses this knowledge
- incorporates explanation processes and ways of handling uncertainty
- typically pertains to problems that can be symbolically represented
- is more forgiving or tolerant of user errors than conventional programs

A typical expert system consists of the knowledge base, the inference engine, and the user interface. The knowledge base is made up of rules and facts that can be drawn upon by the inference engine. The role of the inference engine is to use these facts and rules to draw conclusions based on user inputs. The user interface allows communication between the user and the expert system. This interconnection among user interface, the inference engine, and the knowledge base results in an expert system.

Like everything else, expert systems work best when certain conditions are met:

- at least one acknowledged expert in the area
- sources of the expert's expertise are judgment and experience

- expert is able and willing to explain his knowledge in a systematic way that others can understand
- problem is well-bounded; That is, the problem has an obvious beginning and ending
- problem area has real consensus
- test data is easily available

In developing an expert system, the first step is to select the problem, define the expert system goals, and identify the sources of knowledge. The second step, which is very iterative, is to acquire the knowledge. After the knowledge is gathered and logically organized, it must be programmed using either an expert system application generator, called a shell, or an appropriate programming language.   The next step is validating, testing, and evaluating the system. Validity testing must be done to ensure that the knowledge base and expert system as a whole work as expected. After knowledge refinement, the system must be tested by users working in the expert system's knowledge domain.

The usefulness of any expert system depends on the knowledge and experience of the expert and how faithfully the system mimics the expert's way of thinking.

Expert systems face many of the same requirements as other software systems, including the need to access databases, to interface with software written in traditional languages, and to be portable across platforms.

REASONS FOR DEVELOPING AN EXPERT SYSTEM

- complex problem
- experts are scarce or expensive
- the problem is not complex but repetitive and expensive
- high staff turnover

If the past is any predictor of the future, then libraries in the future will still have repetitive problems and staff turnover. As long as there are libraries there will also be staff training. (For more on training, see the section on Training.)

POSSIBLE AREAS FOR AN EXPERT SYSTEM

Generally, expert systems have been most appropriate in the areas of:

- interpretation
- prediction
- diagnosis
- planning and monitoring
- debugging
- instruction
- control

One of the most highly developed categories is diagnosis. A number of medical researchers and pharmacists have developed systems that doctors use to evaluate rashes, drug reactions, and rare nerve diseases. Such a system asks questions and then presents a list of possible diagnoses. Instruction is obviously the category that would directly benefit libraries and users. We can all think of services, databases, etc., that would benefit from some additional explanation — especially explanations that are site specific. For example, in the Engineering Library we developed an expert system that teaches users how to perform a basic patent search and then connects them with the best database for their search. (This is determined by how they answer a number of questions.) We developed this system because, like many libraries and information centers, we are under increasing pressure to provide more help to all levels of users — from novices to experienced researchers. Another aspect, one that can't be discounted, is that this type of program is available whenever our users need it and can be repeated as often as necessary without its getting tired or crabby.

Possible Library Applications

Library applications fall into two types: "knowledge-rich domains" and "information-rich domains." An example of a knowledge-rich domain is library cataloging and an example of an information-rich domain is patent searching .

CATALOGING

Cataloging and classifying is a ripe area for the development of expert systems. It is rule-based, and the domain is heavily controlled by schedules and tables, so it is not surprising that a number of libraries have been working to develop systems that will help catalogers select records to edit or modify from national databases, such as OCLC, based on locally developed rules. Interestingly, a number of Australian libraries, particularly Monash University Library, have been working in this area. More information on this topic is available in the journal *Library Hi Tech*, (vol .10, nos. 1-2).

Another related example is the development of expert systems in records management. These systems keep track of the various retention rules, guidelines, and management decisions.

REFERENCE SYSTEMS

Several reference systems have been developed in recent years. One with which I am very familiar is *The Patent Information Assistant*. This system was designed to help users navigate the complex and often baffling manual and electronic patent-search tools. Patent searching represents a well-bounded problem — the patron wants information found in a patent or she doesn't. Patent searching also involves expert knowledge, rules of thumb, and experience. Best of all, patent searching is something many users want to do totally on their own, for security reasons. More information on this specific expert system can be found in an article in *Online* (March 1990, pp. 56-66).

Other reference examples are an expert system to help users find specific poems and one that helps users decided which on-line database is the most cost effective for their topic.

INTELLIGENT FRONT AND BACK ENDS

This is an area with real potential for libraries. We have all used systems that would benefit from a library-designed site-specific front end that would give users instruction and would also capture needed accounting or chargeback information. Other systems would benefit from back ends. These could help users parse out bibliographic citations and library catalog records or could provide help with using datasets.

HOW TO GET STARTED — A 12-STEP PROGRAM

Step 1:   Definition
         What do we want and need?
         What is practical?

Step 2:   Project organization
         Who will design it?
         What hardware and software are needed?

Step 3.   Proposal
         Get funding and administrative support

Step 4. Write specifications
Step 5. Design definitions
         Modules, programs, files
         Prototyping
Step 6. Coding
Step 7. Testing individual modules and integration of the modules
Step 8. Documentation
Step 9. Installation
Step 10. Maintenance
Step 11. Enhancement
Step 12. Publicize

Notice how many of the above steps are directly related to traditional library work. The major difference is in coding knowledge, and for this you can rely on a number of packaged shells. Over the last few years many of these have been developed, and most of those that have survived have been reviewed. Good places to look for these reviews are *PC Magazine*, *BYTE*, and other computer magazines.

Also notice that this kind of system requires commitment to maintenance and enhancement. It will no sooner be in and working and someone will say, "Wouldn't it be nice if it could ..." or "This one part isn't quite right."

Summary

Expert systems are just one way to help users navigate between and among the various electronic information access tools. Another way is hypertext or hypercard, and this is discussed in the next chapter.

HYPERTEXT: Hypertext refers to nonsequential reading and writing. A hypertext system is a database management system that allows users to view and make connections between screens of information using associative links   that is, a user showing an interest in one subject is offered optional paths to information on related topics. The systems allow a user to link information quickly and easily along the path of the user's interests. Small discrete units of information may be viewed as needed and also supply cues to take the user to other, related units of information. (In conventional print-based sources, "see" and "see also" notes, as well as footnotes and bibliography entries, supply a related sort of cue.) A well-designed hypertext system encourages users to browse and hunt through the available material and makes them feel that they can move about freely according to their own interests and needs.

HYPERMEDIA: IF THE FOCUS OF A HYPERTEXT PROGRAM IS ON NONTEXTUAL INFORMATION, THE TERM HYPERMEDIA IS OFTEN USED INSTEAD.

Mitchell Brown
McKinney Engineering Library
Technical Assistant
The General Libraries
The University of Texas at Austin
LLMCB@utxdp.dp.utexas.edu

8. The Role of Librarians in Developing Software: Hypertext

Information sources available to microcomputer owners have changed the conventional methods of communicating ideas. Incorporating text, graphics, sound, animation, and video images into communications — as is made possible with hypertext — is a remarkable departure from the traditional two-dimensional space of paper-based print media. Traditionally, access to information in a book has been linear, requiring the user to either scan the pages sequentially to discover its contents or to use an index to isolate a starting point. Now, with a combination of information delivery options (text, audio, motion video), access to information contained in prepared materials can be offered in various ways apart from traditional scanning from beginning to end of source. The ability to make connections between concepts and to communicate by combining media make hypertext and hypermedia powerful information delivery instruments. Ideally, hypertext provides easy access to information in a way that matches the way a person thinks. Additionally, in this ideal picture, a hypertext package provides formats and sources to satisfy a variety of needs, including both quick answers and in-depth explorations. The challenge to librarians and information specialists is to find ways to select from the immense potential of information sources and to develop a product that is useful to users.

Vannevar Bush's 1945 *Atlantic Monthly* article "As We May Think" is credited with originating the idea of hypertext. Bush introduced the idea that, with the expansion of information available, "information overload" would become a serious problem. He advocated an effort to create a mechanical device — which he called "Memex" — that would separate information from the physical location of the original and make it available and useful to a user. Also in the 1940's, work was beginning on a necessary component of creating the reality to match Bush's ideal — a computing language that would allow the connection of portions of programming code to other lines of programming code and also to peripheral devices, such as optical disks and other databases. An early application of the ability to proceed in a nonlinear fashion was for use in computer-based tutorials, where a user can repeat a portion of a lesson until its concepts are mastered.

Bush's broader vision of an interactive linking device for communicating ideas was developed by two researchers, Douglas C. Englebart at the Stanford Research Institute and Theodor Nelson of Xanadu. In 1963 Englebart developed a system he called NLS (ONLine System). NLS contained features that would eventually become part of hypertext, including the use of windows, use of a pointer device (a "mouse"), ability to send messages by electronic mail, and the ability to link and annotate documents in a hypertext-like environment. The term "hypertext" was coined by Theodor Nelson in the 1960s when he used it to describe nonsequential reading and writing that link related passages (or "nodes" or "cards") of text. This innovative approach for addressing programming code was published in *Computer Lib/Dream Machines* in 1974. Developments in computer technology and the introduction of powerful personal microcomputers encouraged exploration of this technique for use on small computer systems. Some hypertext products are purchased as completed programs. More typically, hypertext software is purchased and applications developed by library staff members or others who see a way to enhance a learning experience. Applications include leading students to more information about poets and poetry and giving assistance in finding library locations, and expand considerably beyond this — given the energy and inspiration of would-be creators.

What Does Hypertext Look Like?
Some Examples

In a lecture this would be the time to show an actual demonstration of using hypertext software, but since that will not work here, it's time to show some sample screens. The two examples that follow show aids for getting around in a hypertext program.

To help with use of a complex hypertext-system database, a graphical display feature may be included to serve as a "road map," to show the user his or her location in the system and how to escape or continue.

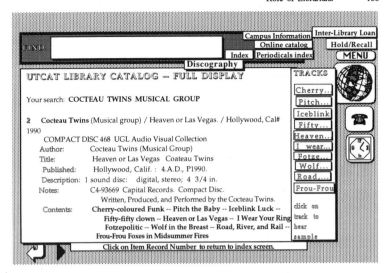

Figure 1. Sample of graphical display with thumbnail-size icons.[1]

The road map may be accomplished in a simple way, such as by showing all the windows displayed in the search in a thumbnail-size picture on one screen. Choosing a displayed icon with the mouse directs the hypertext program to take the user to information in that field.

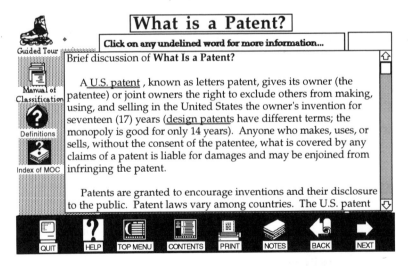

Figure 2. Sample of graphical display with more complicated relational connections.[2]

More complicated displays for guiding users give the appearance of an actual road map. They show where it is possible to go, functioning like a tour map that gives available routes and landmarks to help the traveler, and even showing the user where he or she is on the map. By choosing features from the interface, such as the location of a particular library at the University of Texas at Austin, the hypertext system can provide information on location, collection holdings, hours, and historical anecdotes about the history of the library.

Some Software

Although most hypertext systems have a similar basic architecture, they may vary greatly in the amount of information they are designed to manage and deliver. Also, the manner in which users are allowed to browse the information differs from product to product, as do the techniques used in writing the programming code. For example, the introduction in 1987 of Bill Atkinson's HyperCard is credited with giving a substantial boost to the use of hypertext in multimedia applications. HyperCard made it easier for the constructor of a particular application to incorporate media and enhanced the experience of the end user.

The most divergent feature distinguishing hypertext software is the intended audience for the material and the way the presentation interface is written for that audience. Below are four "classes" of hypertext systems as differentiated by target user group:[3]

- Single-user: Guide, HyperCard, SuperCard
- Multi-user: Intermedia, NoteCards
- Corporate: Augment, Carnegie-Mellon's ZOG
- World: Xanadu

(Note: HyperCard® is a registered trademark of the Claris Corporation. SuperCard® is a registered trademark of the Aldus Corporation.)

Recommendations to Librarians

The features of a hypertext system that appeal to librarians and information professionals are those that lead to what everyone wants in a computer-based product — a product that is easy to use and satisfying for those who use it. For hypertext these features include a good user interface, easily used word processing capabilities, well-developed information trails, sharing between systems, capability for simultaneous use by more than one person, maintenance of an audit trail, a hierarchy of link and node classifications, programming characteristics that encourage making improvements, navigational charts of the system, and character-string searching.

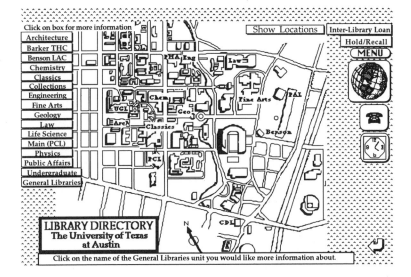

Figure 3. Sample of graphical display with complicated relational connections and with linking to sound sources.[4]

The user interface — the screens of information presented to the user — should be clear and make use of the system seem intuitive. Ideally, the screens will provide a wide flexibility in making choices and allow users to direct their searching. A system should be designed to allow sophisticated users to find the search productive, but also should consider novices' need for a tutorial.

Easily used word processing features allow for modification or annotation of chunks of information and allow users to easily take away information for use elsewhere.

The paths that lead users down information trails should be constructed so that they deliver users where they need to be, while allowing for a variety of access points — rather like designing a building with plenty of doors so that a person coming from any direction can easily get in.

The system should permit copying and sharing of information between users, either on the same system or in different environments, even though the underlying programs may be different for different hypertext applications.

An effective system allows multiple, simultaneous users to access and share the system without inadvertently or maliciously affecting each other's searches.

The hypertext system should provide a history of the actions within a search — similar to an audit trail. This is important for reconstructing a previously used path.

Links to information sites and the information chunks that are located in those sites need a subject heading or brief description of contents to help users make informed decisions about which nodes to open. Also, hierarchically classifying nodes of information — assigning them into levels such as primary, secondary, and tertiary sources — can help keep users from the discouragement that comes with getting bogged down in marginally relevant locations.

The systems should allow for modification or enhancement to better serve the needs of a particular audience. Each hypertext system should ideally contain a tool kit to be used in creating a more highly individualized application of the original.

For more complicated systems, navigational charts are essential. These may appear as graphical interfaces that detail the relationships between major components of a system. Figure 3 is an example of such an interface, allowing user access to text information, motion, and sound (the buttons with song titles are linked to sampled music).

Hypertext systems should allow searching by character string. This is the search strategy most apparent to library users — the phrases and words they think of when describing the subject of interest. An added feature may be a thesaurus that checks for related terms, but the user should be helped and not hindered by the feature.

Limitations and Optimism

While relational paths to information sites can make searching easier, time and effort are required by the librarian to identify and create this linkage. Because multiple paths are available and can become confusing, users of hypertext can suffer disorientation in their searching. Librarians need to go into hypertext projects with a realistic view of what will be required of them and, to help new users, plan to provide tutorial programs and navigational guides. And, no matter how well designed the hypercard product, users will still be required to make judgments about the usefulness of the information retrieved in a search.

This kind of realistic thinking, however, should not detract from the potential and promise of hypertext. As noted earlier, at their best hypertext products match a user's thought processes and make locating information easier; they can enhance learning. The challenge for librarians continues (as it does in other areas of their work) to select the best and make it as useful as possible for the library's clientele.

NOTES:

1. Mitchell Brown, Hypercard card entry in "U.S. Patent Tutorial," using Hypercard 2.0 (Santa Clara, CA: Claris Corp.), 1992. (unpublished)

2. Mitchell Brown, Hypercard entry in "UTCAT Emulation," using Hypercard 2.0 (Santa Clara, CA: Claris Corp.), 1992. (unpublished)

3. Ching-Chih Chen, *Hypersource on Multimedia/Hypermedia Technologies.* (Chicago: Library and Information Technology Association, American Library Association), 1989, p. 4.

4. Mitchell Brown, Hypercard card entry in "UTCAT Emulation," using HyperCard 2.0 (Santa Clara, CA: Claris Corp.), 1992. (unpublished)

VI. ELECTRONIC GEAR

This chapter looks at the numerous technologies that are having an impact on libraries. The term *gear* is used for no particular reason other than that it covers a range of add-on boards and equipment. Some of this gear has been discussed or mentioned in other chapters (e.g., scanners, E-mail, CD-ROM), but other technologies, such as SGML and multimedia, have not. The point here is to illuminate the various technologies.

Susan B. Ardis
Head, McKinney Engineering Library
The General Libraries
The University of Texas
LLSBA@utxdp.dp.utexas.edu

9. FROM CD-ROMs TO VIRTUAL REALITY: A LOOK AT THE TECHNOLOGIES

CD-ROM

CD-ROMs are a direct offshoot of compact digital audio discs . They are also related to interactive and digital video, as well as to optical disks. All these devices store machine-readable digitally encoded information. CD-ROM is not a replacement for computer memory because it is a "write once read many" technology. Instead, it is a low-cost, high-capacity, mass-distribution medium. Today the most common use for CD-ROMs is as an archival distribution and storage medium for large amounts of regularly updated data — such as periodical indexes, atlases, dictionaries, and games. This is because a single disk is the equivalent of:

- 800 eight-inch floppy disks
- 200 books each with 1,000 pages
- 10 magnetic tapes
- 1,500 5¼-inch floppy disks
- 275,000 pages of text.

Up until quite recently most CD-ROM drives were used by businesses and libraries. This is starting to change, as more and more new PCs have been sold with internal CD-ROM drives for use with atlases, games, and dictionaries. Individuals are adding single drives, and libraries are creating larger and larger arrays of drives--or mini-networks (more than one disk) — using jukeboxes , daisy-chaining the drives, or installing LANs.

A daisy chain is nothing more than several CD-ROM players connected together with several workstations. This arrangement allows multiple users of the system, but still only one user per actual disk. Daisy chains have several advantages: they are relatively inexpensive when compared to servers and they are easy to set up, maintain, and run. The disadvantages are lack of remote access and only one user per disk.

Another popular arrangement is the jukebox CD-ROM changer. These are more common in the audio CD world than in the CD-ROM world, but the CD-ROM version provides value on small LANs where users need access to multiple disks. Several different types of devices exist. For example, industrial jukeboxes or minichangers consist of magazines or cartridges, and each one has a read head and several slots for individual disks. Calling them jukeboxes is very apt — one player, many disks, and automatic disk switching, similar to the old Wurlitzer jukeboxes.

The most flexible and expensive option is the LAN CD-ROM network. This one is gaining in popularity in academic libraries. In this setup, the CD-ROM server allows multiple workstations to access simultaneously up to 21 drives per server. The LAN (see LAN chapter for more information) consists of PC workstations, a dedicated server (minimally a 486), a CD-ROM tower, and software such as Novell NetWare to control and run the server. The LAN arrangement has several advantages:

- as many users as workstation PCs
- users may access any disk on the system at any time from any station.
- remote connectivity possible

The major disadvantage is expense. CD-ROM LANs are more expensive to purchase, set up and maintain and they require dedicated and trained programming staff.

One of the holy grails of CD-ROM has been the search for an inexpensive and effective erasable CD-ROM. An erasable disk shares some properties with floppy disks and magnetic tape, in that users can store, retrieve, disseminate, and rewrite computer information. However, one benefit of nonerasable disks is just that — users cannot change, erase, or add information to disks that have an index, such an Inpec, on it.

SUMMARY

Like everything else, CD-ROM has advantages and disadvantages. For now, the best reasons for selecting this technology in a library are:

1. data is archival
2. data needs only periodic updating
3. distribution for large amounts of data is economical
4. information is available locally
5. budgeting is a local matter

For individuals and power users, the reasons are similar, but one major advantage is cost. CD-ROM drives for individual PCs are now quite moderate in price, and the cost of games, atlases, and dictionaries is also quite moderate. However, the same is not true for periodical indexes, and many users are surprised when they discover how expensive these are. Users don't realize that in a library the continuing cost of the disks is the real expense — not the equipment. This expense, both the direct costs and labor, is what is driving many libraries to networking--it is just not economically sound to purchase, install, and maintain periodical indexes on CD-ROM for every workstation.

FAX

What surprises many people is that the fax machine, that office necessity, is now 150 years old. It was patented in England on May 27, 1843, by Alexander Bain. This makes the fax machine 30 years older than the telephone. While the telephone quickly became an office and home necessity, the fax machine didn't become popular until the 1980s. Several reasons account for this, but mainly, the marketplace could not see a reason to send typewritten information over a telephone line. It was the Japanese who saw the benefit--fax was cheaper than character typewriters.

The basic principle behind fax technology is quite simple: today's machine separates the image to be sent into fine lines and then divides each line into white and black portions that can be sent over a telephone line as electrical impulses. In Bain's original machine the image was broken down into the dots and dashes of Morse code. Although his invention was brilliant, Bain never really developed it because it was so much slower than sending a telegram using Morse code directly. The next development (and one that also made photocopiers possible) happened in 1878, when it was discovered that selenium's electrical resistance falls when light shines on it. This meant that electrical impulses could be used to put ink on a piece of paper in a controlled pattern. It was then possible to send electrical impulses over a wire to a machine that would translate them into heat. The heat would make a pattern on a piece of thermal-sensitive paper.

This invention waited until the marketplace was ready for it. Once the Japanese developed an inexpensive and reliable machine, the fax machine's other strength became obvious: because it is attached to telephone lines, fax is internationally compatible and is very simple to use. So even with complex digital data compression and circuitry, all it really takes to operate a fax is a fax phone number, a message to send, and the push of a button. Very little other computer technology is quite this user-friendly.

The effects of the fax machine have been enormous: it permits fast, inexpensive, and accurate transmission of engineering drawings, specifications, contracts, bid requirements, interlibrary loan forms, and journal articles all over the world. Fax has literally changed the world. With access to fax, individuals can send messages to their congressmen or even the president. One demonstration of the power of the fax was when the Chinese dissidents sent information about Tiananmen Square quickly to Chinese students studying all over the world.

It didn't take too long for users to realize that it would be very convenient to send and receive fax messages via their computers. This led to the development of fax modems — devices that can send computer data and text over a telephone line to another computer with a fax modem or to a stand-alone fax. The fax modem turns a PC into a real workstation — one that can connect to the Internet, a stand-alone fax , or a computer with a fax.

As wonderful as fax modems are they do have problems. First, not all fax modems communicate with computers using the same standard and, second, a fax modem by itself cannot scan a journal article, a handwritten note, or any document not in a computer file. In terms of communications, there are two basic standards:

1. Class 1, which is basically the Hayes modem standard applied to fax machines
2. CAS, or computer applications specifications. CAS is an interface between the fax software and the fax modem. It basically allows the collecting and queuing of fax messages for transmission.

In terms of scanned images, computer users who want to use their fax modems for this purpose need to also add a scanner (see Scanners in this section). If they want to edit someone else's message, they will also need a digital scanner--a scanner that converts the image into a form the computer can use--not just an image or picture of the document.

Summary

Often, the software that comes with the fax modem is weak, so you need to consider purchasing a separate program. Any fax modem should support the following features:

1. single and multiple-page cover sheets
2. faxing from an application (word processing or spreadsheet, e.g.)
3. unattended faxing
4. compatibility with available printers
5. ability to manage faxes by filing, deleting, compressing, and printing

Since most fax modems save messages in proprietary formats, make sure that the software includes a conversion utility. For example, OCR (optical character recognition) capability is useful in converting faxes to editable text. See *PC Magazine,* December 8, 1992, for a review and comparison of 13 fax software products.

When operating a fax modem on your computer you should consider installing a "smart line," especially if you have a limited number of phone lines. This $50 to $100 device monitors incoming phone calls and determines whether a call is for a person or a fax machine. Many organizations don't need a dedicated phone just for the fax. Some fax modems have the "smart line" feature built in--most do not.

In a way fax is working against the "paperless" office. A faxed note, often handwritten, including drawings or other graphics, often produces a paper copy in a form that is incompatible with computerization. E-mail is an obvious competitor for many types of communication because it sends a digital message (see E-mail). But E-mail does not send graphics or images with the ease of a fax. In the near future neither technology will drive out the other.

Scanners

Up until quite recently, full-page or flatbed gray-scale scanners were expensive and slow; this is beginning to change. A fax or image scanner is really nothing more than a sealed box containing a fluorescent or incandescent light bulb that illuminates the target or image to be scanned, a charge-coupled device (CCD), and a photosensor that absorbs the image's reflected light. The CCD is essentially a photocopier with an array of thousands of light-detecting cells that produce a variable voltage level proportional to the amount of light reflected. Scanners associated with telephones (faxes) then pass the signal to a device that sends it out over the phone. Image scanners with an analog-to-digital converter process these same voltages into digital values that are transmitted to a computer interface card--and the image is "sent" to a PC.

It is important to note that images hog both disk and memory. The amount of space consumed depends on several factors: size of the image, number of shades of gray, and resolution. A standard 4 by 4 scanned image can, depending on the amount of gray scanned, take anywhere between 200KB and 1.9MB of storage.

Whether you intend to fax, print, or store your images for later use, you will have a number of format decisions to make (see the section on Indexing for intellectual decisions). The most common software for scanners is Tagged Image File Format. TIFF files can store both 1-bit black-and-white and 8-bit gray-scale images. Other popular formats are PCX, GIF, and EPS. PCX is popular because it supports up to 256 gray scales and it can be read by Microsoft Windows. CompuServe's Graphics Interchange Format (GIF) internally compresses image files, while EPS (Encapsulated PostScript) is the publishing-industry's standard because it can accept gray-scale, bit-maps, and vector information.

Considerations for scanner selection:

- compatibility with Hewlett-Packard's Scanjet since this is one of the most common scanners
- ability to send output directly to a file in a variety of formats, including EPS and TIFF
- automatic document feeder capable of handling various paper thickness
- compare scanning speed for entire process not just time it takes to input the image

By combining a page scanner with low-cost document-image-processing software and hardware, it is now possible to develop a system for handling the large amount of paper and electronic documents now being used in libraries. Some possible applications include engineering notebooks, standards, schematics, and, in academic libraries, homework on reserve.

Electronic Mail or E-mail

Electronic mail or E-mail has entered the mainstream of corporate and library life to such a degree than many people take it for granted. The most common use of E-mail is to send short text messages. Increasingly, however, these systems are being used to send more than just text; they are being used to send electronic documents, financial transactions, and data. E-mail is now the single most visible application of distributed computing. It is the first application that is available to all computer users regardless of their technical expertise.

E-mail is based on the idea that when any two computers can exchange information this information can be formatted so that humans can read it. E-mail's great success is that it encourages the simultaneous flow of information to many geographically dispersed people.

E-mail has several advantages over the telephone — messages can be in-depth and read at the reader's convenience, and message tag is not a problem. However, for now, E-mail does have one real disadvantage over the telephone--not all E-mail systems are connected to each other. They must be able to send E-mail worldwide to users regardless of whether they are connected to the Internet, CompuServe, or a company E-mail system. E-mail users are demanding universal seamless connectivity comparable to that of the telephone system.

PABX

PABX is what used to be called a switchboard. Switchboards became PBXes (Private Branch Exchanges) when manufacturers began to use computers to connect telephone extensions to each other and to the outside world. PBXes of recent vintage are often called PABX systems, with the A standing for Automatic. Sometimes they are called CBXes (Computerized Branch Exchanges).

The easiest way to conceptualize a PABX is as a single large switch. The standard office button telephones (also known as key sets) contain their own switching circuitry. In a PABX system all those buttons are relocated in one large centralized switch, shared by all phones in the system. A PABX allows multiple in-house telephones to be served by outgoing trunk lines . (A trunk line is the external line that runs from the organization to the local telephone company.) Unlike key (button) systems, where the user selects the line by pushing the button, the PABX automatically chooses the line for an outgoing call and also coordinates all incoming calls to prevent unnecessary tie-ups and busy signals. In effect, the PABX acts as a telephone traffic controller.

PABXes can be particularly cost-effect for libraries with large numbers of telephones or those with the need for various features, such as voice mail. Another advantage is that these systems are easier to reconfigure--numbers can be changed, phones relocated, and new lines added more quickly than with ordinary telephones. All these changes are made through programming. One of the most interesting for libraries is electronic voice messaging or voice mail.

Voice Mail

Voice mail can be purchased as part of a larger organization's telephone system or it can be PC-based. To use such systems libraries must have telephones with individual numbers (PBAX or single lines — no key sets). Voice mail systems allow users to call one number and be routed to the correct telephone. They can be as sophisticated or simple as needed. Many of the simplest are the most user friendly, and route calls to very few other phones. Generally, users complain if they have to listen to and remember too many choices from a menu. However, these systems provide users with basic information such as hours, location, and messaging at all hours of the day. For example, in one Patent Depository library, inventors can call at any time and get a message that defines the most common kinds of intellectual property, gives basic protection for each, and provides referrals for more information.

Voice mail's big advantage over E-mail is that almost everyone has a telephone--not everyone has a computer and a modem.

Wireless LAN

One of the newest hot topics on the electronic horizon is the wireless LAN (see LAN section for more information on wired LANs). Just when libraries were beginning to be connected and interconnected, now such companies as AT&T, Motorola, National Semiconductor, and Apple, are pursuing the wireless LAN and the wireless WAN as alternative solutions to the problems posed by hardwired networks. Hardwired networks within a building can consist of several wiring types: twisted-pair, coaxial, and fiber-optic cabling . All of these are difficult and expensive to install, maintain, and change. A wireless network, on the other hand, is generally linked through radio waves, cellular telephones, or infrared light using cellular telephone technology. As with FM radio and cellular telephones, information on a wireless LAN would be available to anyone with the right receiver and within range of the transmitter. You can see how exciting the idea of wireless networks would be. They would be easy to change, cheap to maintain, and installation — well this could be a breeze.

Office worker mobility and the expense of keeping workers connected today is not a trivial expense or problem, and the problem will only grow as libraries become more and more electronic. According to *Electronic Design* (March 19, 1992, p. 51), over one-half of office workers with PCs will move annually and it is estimated that data terminals move as often as 1.5 to 3 times per year with "an estimated cost of $200 to $1000 per wiring change." Given the expense, the loss of productivity due to downtime for recabling and the time often needed to resolve cross-talk, impedance matching, and data security issues, it is no wonder that some see the use of electromagnetic energy to transmit data as a possible alternative.

Worker mobility also takes another form--workers traveling and using their notebook computers. Many corporate travelers are eager to receive and send data through their laptops and notebook computers without being tied to a telephone line. Often they are not near a telephone, much less a pay phone with plug-in facilities. Wireless data transfer technology would solve this problem and let users communicate from cars, airports, and street corners. This is the dream of many computer users--to be untethered and roam the LAN's domain without losing connection to their application.

Actually this is not really a new idea, because wireless point-to-point modems with ranges of up to 10 miles have been on sale since the early 1980s. In fact wireless point-to-point modems have been successfully used by Federal Express and many police and fire departments. Will wireless communication become as ubiquitous as the portable pager? Probably, and when it does, it will definitely have an impact on libraries and information delivery. Users will be able to communicate with the library's network and receive downloaded information wherever they are, just as salespeople will be able to get schematics, prices, and specifications. So the library without walls could also become the library without wires.

Multimedia Technology

Historically, computers were designed to work with relatively simple information such as numbers and letters. But in the last decade graphics information has been added. Now the task is to develop computer multimedia technology that will handle still or moving images and sound, and will facilitate user interaction. Many organizations and companies, such as the Department of Defense, American Airlines, and Domino's Pizza, are interested in developing interactive multimedia programs that could be used for training employees. Others are interested in developing business presentations, merchandising, and public information kiosks.

What exactly is multimedia? Multimedia can be broken into four areas: audio, high-capacity storage, video, and networking. Because audio data is easier to work with, you can expect to see more audio-enabled hardware and software. Audio is also affordable, because computer sound was adopted by the video-game industry. Today's computer sound boards come equipped with both recording and playback features and a MIDI (musical instrument digital interface). This is a very hot area — in 1993 experts predict that over 2.5 million add-on sound boards will be shipped. As a result, software is starting to take advantage of audio. For instance, when Lotus Sound is combined with a sound board, users can apply voice annotations to various applications, such as spreadsheets, word processing, and E-mail. Other companies, including Microsoft and Apple, are also working on sound. Microsoft is modifying its Windows program so that it will handle audio as well as video, and Apple's Macintosh already supports sound. For example, soon we will be able to buy dictionaries that pronounce the looked-up word or ones that read entries for the print handicapped.

All is not rosy however. One problem continues to be the amount of data storage that is consumed by sound. As a result, for the foreseeable future, the best way to store sound will be on CD-ROM because a disc has 650 MB (megabytes) of storage and can easily and affordably handle audio. The other related technologies, erasable optical drives, which use laser beams to read and write, and videodiscs are still too expensive to produce and master for widespread use.

Full-motion video is the most demanding area of multimedia. Each second consumes 22.1 MB of storage and requires a network bandwidth of 178.8 Megabits. This means that a 650 MB drive can store only 30 seconds of uncompressed video, and the situation is not much different for still or single pictures. Not too surprisingly, a lot of research is going into solutions to the storage problems. One of the most interesting is the development of data compression and decompression techniques.

SUMMARY

Unfortunately, today's computer networks and servers are designed for small-packet asynchronous data communication rather than the synchronous services needed by multimedia. Still, applications will drive development. Possible applications for libraries include just-in-time training, where training videos are stored on a server and workers can get up-to-date training as needed. Another area of interest is the information kiosk, a place where users can get a wide variety of information, directions, and help. The University of Texas is currently working on information and direction kiosks that will be all over campus. Users will be able to find departmental addresses and locations on a map, listings for university programs from concerts to short courses, as well as the library's on-line catalog and each library location and hours. Other education applications include customized course work. The St. Louis Zoo is developing a multimedia computer system. This will provide teachers with videos, sounds, text, and slides on biology, ecology, and conservation.

Videoconferencing

Why hold a videoconference instead of a conference phone call? Probably for the same reason that you call a meeting rather than conduct it over the phone or by E-mail. The participants need to see each other and evaluate body language for real understanding. An economic solution to the meeting problem is videoconferencing.

Videoconferencing or teleconferencing has been around for quite a while, but the equipment has been fairly expensive. This is changing; interactive low-cost digital equipment that can be plugged in and operated easily is now available, and new telephone technology is improving transmission and audio reception.

Economy is not the only advantage of digital videoconferencing — others are its portability, its on-tap availability, and its ability to handle slides, videos, and overheads. Phone compatibility makes it possible to transmit rather than broadcast. As a result, hooking up is more like making a long-distance telephone call instead of engineering a cross-country television hookup.

Some stumbling blocks remain. One is that 95% of today's videoconferences are within organizations and most are on proprietary equipment. This means that company A often cannot talk to company B because of dissimilar compression algorithms, mixed public and private networks, and lack of interoperability for speeds and carriers. But work on this problem is progressing by vendors such as PictureTel, NEC, Mitsubishi, VTEL, and BT North America. The vendors are also working on the concept of "desktop" videoconferencing. This is the future, but questions remain:

- What interface is best with the public network?
- Can compatibility be established between different switching and operating systems?
- Does desktop videoconferencing belong in a LAN/WAN environment?

The whole LAN/WAN question is problematic. Simple logic might lead to the conclusion that since LANs already link workstations, LANs should link desktop videoconferencing. A number of problems need to be solved before real-time conferencing is available on your local LAN. Because LANs are:

- the cause of delays
- optimized for bursts of activity
- expensive to maintain and upgrade.

LAN users can deal with this for packet-type information such as E-mail, CD-ROM indexes, or parts lists. However, videoconferencing must be smooth like a face-to-face meeting or telephone call--not jerky and bumpy like E-mail.

Videoconferencing has ramifications for libraries. It is the rare library that can send staff to even important, much less, interesting meetings. Videoconferencing would make it possible for more people to attended meetings, without taking a big bite out of their work schedule or the travel budget. Videoconferencing may just be the next technology to get the wide library acceptance accorded the photocopier, the fax, and the CD-ROM. This technology may add to our warehouse of more and better information sources.

SGML

A little while back when the word *document* was used as a noun, it conjured up images of reports and legal papers from various governmental agencies. Today the word also encompasses E-mail, faxes, journal articles, user's manuals, and notices from electronic bulletin boards. All these kinds of documents share a common inheritance--the use of organizing themes that relate to the origin of the document--books are with books, journals with journals, E-mail with E-mail, and so on.

The challenge now is to devise a way to transform the information in all these documents so that it can be transmitted from one place to another. This means that documents must share an organization based on information transmission rather than on their physical arrangement. What is needed is a way of creating context-free documents--in other words, giving information a form that is transportable and not linked to any particular document style, software, or hardware. One way of doing this is to develop a standardized mark-up language.

In the world of publishing, *mark-up* refers to the typographic specifications and other presentation instructions that are marked on a manuscript befor it goes to a typesetter or printer. In the electronic world, mark-up refers to electronic tags or codes interspersed in the text. In either case, mark-up separates a document's elements into logical divisions and then specifies how those divisions will look. In the past this mark-up was printer or product specific. For example, when you use Microsoft word, your document is displayed on the screen as WYSIWYG (what you see is what you get). You do not see the specific proprietary codes or tags used to produce the desired effect--you see only the effect..

Generally mark-up comes in two types: descriptive and procedural. Descriptive mark-up identifies logical units, say chapter headings, but it does not address how the final document will look. Procedural mark-up tells what action is to be performed on the document's content to achieve the desired appearance of the text. An example of descriptive mark-up is *chapnum=Chapter Thirteen*, and an example of procedural mark-up is *down 10; center; 12pt.* Both are in essence style sheets that simplify printing and layout. Notice that neither describes the document's content.

Electronic-publishing systems, full-text databases, hypertext and other document oriented files require both content mark-up and traditional mark-up. This need has led to the development of new kinds of mark-up languages that describe content in a way that is not related to how the information is presented on the page or the screen. One of the better known and most promising mark-up languages is SGML (Standard Generalized Markup Language).

SGML may be one of the most important steps on the road to the truly interconnected paperless world. SGML is an attempt to produce publications that are not tied to any particular software or printer. When a document is produced using SGML, instead of a paper document or word processing file, the document is produced in ASCII text and all formatting information is in ASCII tags, inserted between angle brackets < >. This means that a publication using SGML can be sent to any printer, screen, speech synthesizer, automatic translator, or storage device. This is because the document's codes and tags now identify the logical and structural components, not the specific typefaces, fonts, sizes, margins, tabs, etc. Translation of the mark-up codes happens when the mark-up is run through a selected output device. This device, say a printer, then consults a dictionary of Document Type Definitions (DTDs) and decides what combination of screen or printer instructions should be attached. For example, the main title of this section, Electronic Gear, instead of being procedurally coded as Times Roman 14pt centered bold, would be coded in SGML as <maintitle>; The second-tier heading-- Scanner-- would be <2ndhead> and so on throughout the text. As a result, different printers could use different DTDs to produce different effects--but, in every document, maintitles could be retrieved, whatever final printer format was selected.

Documents, whether electronic or paper, create problems. The real problem with both is not the number of file cabinets or the amount of computer storage space needed. The real problem is that paper and electronic files trap and hide information and know-how. They are disorganized, and too often the needed electronic information is there but spread out over a number of platforms, in files, directories, or LANs. SGML may be a way out of this mess because documents coded using it could be transferred from any computer file to another.

Currently, the Department of Defense is very interested in SGML. One application under review is to have all of its relevant naval contractor files coded in SGML and then satellite download these to on-ship workstations. These files would include text, formulas, illustrations, and provisions for a user notes field. This would serve two purposes: it would save carrying 5 tons of manuals on a 90-ton vessel and provide the ship with up-to-date technical information..

With a standardized mark-up language, developers and system integrators could manage large numbers of documents and exchange information among the various hardware and software platforms without expensive conversion. The library and information applications of something like SGML are enormous.

Virtual Reality

The reality a lot of people are talking about is virtual reality and how it will impact on libraries — electronic or otherwise. What exactly is virtual reality? Virtual reality (VR) uses visual, auditory, and other stimuli to synthetically generate an environment. In other words, you don't just sit in front of a computer screen but instead enter a "world." That world that is a three-dimensional environment that can be manipulated directly and in such a way that you are unaware of interacting with a computer. For example, in a virtual reality room you can walk around, and you can look out the window and see the view. You can use your hands to pick up a cat or move an object from one place to another. You don't need to use a mouse, a joystick, or a keyboard. You will simply don a head-mounted display device and a special glove.

Some examples of virtual reality applications that are already under development are the following:

- architects putting on head-mounted displays and sitting in real wheelchairs to move through a computer-generated apartment interior to check handicapped accessibility
- engineers at Boeing donning a helmet with 3-D display and "entering" a computer-generated model of a lunar rover to check the ergonomics of their design
- doctors practicing a surgical procedure with "virtual surgery"
- U.S. Air Force fighter pilots training to fly

While most of these realities are still fairly crude, many predict that it is in the entertainment world that "serious" technical applications will be developed. Some of the hurdles to be overcome include better tracking, display, and image-generation devices. And finally, like many graphics-intensive applications, VR requires massive computing and storage capabilities. Probably the reality most people will see first is "augmented" reality, and this is also the area with the most potential for library application. In an augmented reality, computer-generated images are superimposed on the user's real world. For example, electricians could walk around the library and see the wiring behind the walls instead of deciphering blueprints.

Probably the "librarian with x-ray vision" will be much easier to find in a comic book or video game than in any near future library. Many of us object to the stereotype, Marion the librarian with a bun--how many of us will want to wear a helmet to do our job? Goggles maybe--but helmets?

VII. IMAGING SYSTEMS

This section is about imaging, an up-and-coming technology that could change libraries and offices more than anything since the telephone. Even with networks, databases, and E-mail, offices and libraries are still in the paper storage and retrieval business. Until recently most organizations had very little staff expertise in imaging even though one of the most commonly available imaging systems is computer-aided design. CAD has been liberating engineers and designers from the drafting tables, but unfortunately it has done little to reduce their dependency on filing cabinets. But things are beginning to change as companies and vendors integrate scanners, conversion software, and retrieval systems into management systems that are capable of organizing all kinds of paper documents, including engineering drawings, working papers, internal reports, notebooks, and blueprints. Imaging systems could integrate aspects of data processing, records management, and office administration into a package that provides quick and easy access to pictorial images, data, and text.

The need to organize this kind of information is best demonstrated by what is happening on the aircraft carrier USS *Forrestal*. Modernization and refitting of this carrier requires almost 1,500 blueprints and countless specifications, notes, and instructions, all developed over many years. Blueprints or plans for a carrier are often large — the largest is E-size, or 19 feet by 40 inches — and out of a thousand plans, a mechanic may need only two. To solve this problem, the Philadelphia naval yard is raster-scanning all these documents and storing them on six CDC disk drives accessed by a minicomputer. When shipworkers need a drawing, the electronic drawing files are transferred to an Interleaf technical publishing system running on Sun Microsystems Sarc Stations. The Interleaf system is used to break drawings down into 11-by-17 inch pages. An E-size drawing requires 27 such pages. It is estimated that the technical schematics for the *Forrestal* will fill 70,000 pages. The advantage of this system is that each page can be copied individually and routed to the proper workgroups when needed, as many times as needed, and as often as needed.

The naval shipyard is facing a problem common to many businesses and libraries that have been in operation for a long time: how can they manage the thousands of documents accumulated over the years? Many technology gurus prognosticate that imaging will be *the* next development in information delivery. Why? The following articles by Stephanie Smith and Susan Cisco should give us some answers.

Stephanie Smith
Systems librarian
Software Technology Branch NASA-JSC
SSMITH@algol.jsc.nasa.gov

10. Picture This...

The information sector is wired in and on-line; we use PCs, fax machines, and CD-ROMs, and we network through the Internet. Amazingly, we're still up to our eyeballs in paper! Think back to the early 1980s, when personal computing was a gleam in a manufacturer's eye. One of the carrots offered to tempt us into the silicon world was the notion of a paperless office. A paperless office? Not mine, how about yours? How about your company? Are even 25% of the documents your company produces on-line? Here we are in the early 1990s and U.S. businesses are churning out 24 million documents and 234 million photocopies a day (Knack). Instead of reducing paper, computers have enabled us to generate more. An Association for Information and Image Management study cites that 95% of the information stored by U.S. businesses is still on paper and that only 1% is on-line in any form, with the remaining 4% on microfilm or on off-line magnetic media (AIIM, 1987). Pictures of harried workers swamped by paper in those ubiquitous articles about the "information glut" aren't too far from the literal truth.

These statistics bear witness to the fact that not much company information is on-line. Yet. Many businesses are in the process of purchasing document-imaging systems and converting their documents and images to digital formats. A Deloitte Touche study placed industry sales for document-imaging systems at $4.8 billion by 1996 (Wolk). The amount of internal on-line company information will continue to increase as technical issues are resolved, business acumen increases- and last but not least, increased profits are realized through streamlined operations, improved efficiency, and better customer service.

The potential role of an information specialist in this emerging environment is particularly interesting. Thornton May, director of research at Tenex Consulting, states that "the indisputable strength of imaging is that it lets you codify, distribute, and manipulate a much larger percentage of your corporate intellectual assets. The bad news is, most organizations don't know how to capture economic value from their intellectual assets" (Wallace). Practiced in the art of codifying, distributing, and manipulating intellectual assets from the centralized position of the company library, librarians can build a strong business case to justify the expense of a document image library accessible throughout the company network. Armed with facts illustrating the advantages of high-density storage, electronic access and delivery of information, data integrity, security, and simultaneous access, you can market your department as the logical location to leverage your company's assets for economic gain. To familiarize you with this emerging technology and perhaps assist you in building your own business case, this chapter presents a high-level overview of the issues involved in the implementation of an imaging system. Items for your consideration include the problem statement, a situation analysis, and the components of an imaging system.

I've already touched on one   problem in today's workplace and workflow: too much paper making its way from my desk, to yours, to the engineer down in development, over to manufacturing, and on and on. Clearly, there is an excess of paper in the workplace, and many studies have been done that quantify this. In addition to the 24 million documents and 234 million photocopies American businesses put out daily, the average worker generates 45 pieces of paper a day. This is folded into the $100 million in cost to corporate American for maintenance of the paper life cycle (Knack).

Consider the life of a document as it works its way through the company. Whether it is an active or legacy document, it must be codified, handled, and routed. The document may need modification or require supporting reports that must be located and collected. At any point along the way it could be folded, spindled, mutilated, lost, misfiled, or waylaid. Unless photocopied, physical documents are available to only one person at a time. To locate a document in mid-processing is difficult and its handles for retrieval are inefficient and time consuming. Added to this ineffectual and expensive process are the space and maintenance needed to store documents for what might be a very long time. To understand this situation more clearly, trace one of your company's internal technical reports from the originator, through all the steps, to your library. Once you have an idea about the cost of the intellectual asset up to that point, add in the cost of integrating it into your collection and storing it for posterity. Multiply this by the number of reports you estimate your company produces. Quite a figure, eh?

Think about the same document being made accessible from a document-imaging platform mounted on a company network. Utilizing an indexing or database schema, documents can be codified and assigned attributes based on a number of criteria and/or be full-text searched. Original and supporting documents can be located in many folders simultaneously, gathered by specific attributes, and accessed by many users at the same time. The handling and misplacement of documents is reduced, and documents can be distributed on a need-to-know basis using security features. The electronic storage of documents and graphical images reduces the time spent looking for items, the physical labor required to move items around, and the amount of storage space items take up in the workplace. Given that many records should be physically retained for specified periods of time, access and proximity to an item can be as close as your local networked computer.

Some imaging systems recreate the office with "electronic file cabinets" that group documents together and place them in folders by an identifying element such as client or case number. Typically documents are scanned in and stored in mass-storage devices called jukeboxes that play CD-ROM like the Wurlitzer at your favorite bar. The main focus in this situation is the mass storage and retrieval of static scanned information. Individual documents can be placed in many folders on a stand-alone workstation or accessed locally, remotely, and simultaneously over a network. The documents can be retrieved by their attributes, distributed, made secure, and are less likely to be lost or damaged.

Another application of imaging systems is oriented around the workflow process that marries the database of scanned documents containing individual customer or product datasets to the business process of forms, editing, redlining and routing. Scanned documents or forms are routed and distributed on the network to multiple employees based on factors such as required transactions, lines of approval, deadlines, and security.

The software used to scan the information is important when data needs to be modified. Various OCR (optical character recognition) software packages can convert images into ASCII characters that can be changed and then resaved as an image. Permission to change or modify original documents can be granted to authorized personnel using various configuration management features. Workflow software often changes the work process itself as bottlenecks and inefficiencies are discovered.

Another scenario for using imaging technology is based on integrating the image system into a larger enterprise-wide information management scheme that includes other important information sources such as E-mail, spreadsheets, databases, and word processed documents. The progression away from task-oriented applications to enterprise imaging signals a new level of evolution for imaging technology and its acceptance in the corporate world. The enterprise library offers a logical view of PC files and allows authorized users to access shared information sources. The accuracy and integrity of data can be maintained with revision rules, and audit trails can be reviewed. Information can also progress through archival stages, with the most important information stored on-line and less accessed information stored on optical disks. The enterprise library can integrate document management, publishing, document imaging, workflow and legacy applications all under one system.

Depending on your company's size and condition you probably have an idea what level of implementation imaging might take in your setting (if any at all). Whether you're simply setting up some mass storage for information, or as part of an enterprise-wide resource you must plan ahead, you must understand your business requirements, the current state of technology and workflow in your company, and be reasonably knowledgeable about current document management technology to create a successful plan for implementing the imaging system that's right for your situation. At a departmental level, you and your staff will probably perform the requirements analysis and write the specifications for your system. At the enterprise level, MIS (management information systems) or an external systems integrator might be called upon to perform these tasks. As an information specialist your knowledge of the corporate information flow is a valuable asset to any of these committees and necessary for assessment and planning strategies. Get involved in this planning process if it's being conducted at the enterprise level.

The goal of implementing an electronic management system is to support the business mission. Once you're clear about the requirements of your business you can begin to develop an approach to satisfying those needs. To determine your system requirements, perform a thorough and comprehensive identification of your present document management scheme. Examine tasks at different stages within the workflow, such as how information is managed and routed, where efforts are duplicated, and where bottlenecks occur. Take note of the workflow volume and types of physical documents people are handling, as well as the retrieval mechanisms used to locate the documents. What exactly are workers extracting from the documents they handle, and what methods are used to gain intellectual access to information within the documents? Depending on the information desired from a document, the image database might be image files indexed by a database of attributes or documents that are available by full-text retrieval or both. These issues will drive the specifications for the software that's used to retrieve data and the hardware storage requirements once it's a digital document.

Evaluate the type and nature of existing electronic tools, such as PCs, networks, E-mail, and operating systems. Interview key personnel concerning work practices and solicit their opinions of more efficient procedures while you analyze the information management system. You'll probably get good ideas about how business should be conducted and gather support on the way. Consider how many people will be affected by the potential system, their level of computer savvy, and possible needs for training. The workflow analysis can lead to a re-engineering of work processes, so even if you can't convince management to shell out for some hardware, you will have identified and hopefully rectified some unproductive work procedures.

Additional analysis of the physical documents themselves is necessary to plan a document conversion process. Record the types and locations of documents, the approximate number and pages of documents and their physical characteristics. What you need to quantify is the volume of documents that need to be converted and the requirements for scanning these documents into the system. What types of documents will be converted? Are the documents of a similar size and color? Do they have staples? Are the pages printed on front and back? The more human intervention required for document conversion from paper to digital form, the higher the price per document. Investigate and compare the cost of an in-house conversion process with that of a service bureau geared up for high-volume conversions. Service bureaus will contract to convert various types of media, such as paper, microfiche, or E-size drawings, into the digital/optical media of your choice. The conversion of an existing database, legacy documents, and incoming information are important items for your analysis as conversion will consume a considerable amount of time and money when you eventually implement your system. Gathering this information may be an arduous task for you or the core team assigned to it, but this kind of in-depth strategic planning will help ensure the successful deployment and desired benefits of the system.

Once you know your business needs and your document management scheme, you're ready to consider some hardware and software issues. You want to shop for a system that's full of "ables"; one that is scalable, portable, interoperable, and flexible. Scalable, so you can grow the system as your business grows; portable, to run across all three platforms — PC, Mac, and UNIX; interoperable, so applications can exchange and use information; and flexible, so you can integrate other applications as needed. The level of support and maintenance the system requires will depend on the complexity of the system you select. The hardware will possibly require special installation personnel and you'll need to provide for system administration. And of course you have somewhere to park this stuff, right?

There are plenty of vendors ready to sell you any and all of their products, so after you've done some research, call up the ones that look like a good match and take advantage of their enthusiasm to demonstrate their products for you. The two main camps in the sales arena are the image vendors, who sell a total imaging package or modules of packages that can be put together incrementally, and the system integrators, who look over your present hardware, document flow and processes, and make recommendations on the re-engineering of those processes and/or system solutions to do the job. Image vendors will generally offer their own commercial off the shelf (COTS) product, possibly in conjunction with another vendor that they've struck a licensing deal with. System integrators may offer you a COTS solution, a custom-developed solution, or a combination of the two glued together with their own code.

The COTS products are pretty easy to check in the current literature for functionality and benchmarks, and you can ask vendors to demonstrate or set up a system at your location so you can take it for a test drive. You can also ask the vendor for a client list and client testimonials. If your application is very specific to your industry and COTS products don't completely meet the bill, you may need a custom-tailored system. A custom system usually has the hardware and software bundled into one package and has all the generic capabilities of a COTS product plus varying degrees of functionality. On the plus side, a tailored system offers flexibility, control, precision, and reduced distribution costs. The negative aspects to remember are that the system is proprietary, complex, may or may not comply with standards, and may not support product integration.

Imaging systems fall into four basic configuration categories, depending upon the degree of implementation: a stand-alone system in one unit; a small stand-alone system with storage peripherals; a LAN system with storage peripherals; and distributed systems on minis or mainframes with various combinations of peripherals. The common elements in any of these systems are document input, storage, document retrieval, and output devices.

Information enters electronic systems in several ways. From the standpoint of work required, the optimal entry into the system is as a native electronic document. The effort required to bring the document on-line is the time it takes to index the items for future retrieval and placement on a storage device. Another way information can be entered into the system is to send the computer a fax of the document. Many packages support fax boards or fax modems. A more common entry point into an imaging system is through a scanning device.

A scanner works by shining a light on a document and registering the light that bounces back. The dark areas on the document reflect less light, and the scanner records the areas of lightness and darkness. The light and dark measurements are converted into digital information and are dependent on whether the document is black and white, gray-scale, or color. After the digital information is created, the processed image is sent to the monitor for display. Color documents are scanned three times, through red, green, and blue filters. After the three scans, the images are combined to form the complete image. The scanner analyzes the dots on the page, and the number of dots measured per inch is called the resolution. Levels of resolution range from 50 to 800 dots per inch. The greater the number of dots the better the picture quality and the higher the resolution.

Scanners are judged by scan rates, resolution, and the image enhancement abilities of the software. When you compare scanner features, pull out your document conversion analysis and match up what you really have to scan with the right kind of scanner. A scanner might have a scan rate that's out of this world, but if the paper has to be continually handled by a person, that time and effort (read $$$) is a factor in the conversion scheme. Other costs associated with scanning are verification of scanned documents, indexing documents, and rescanning documents that were not scanned successfully the first time around. Issues to consider regarding the software that drives the scanner include the ability to group pages as one document and whether you want to capture data in an ASCII format or as a bit-mapped image.

The information that's imported into the system has to be stored in primary, secondary, or tertiary storage. These storage devices are ranked by access time, capacity, and cost. The general rule of thumb is that as you decrease access speed, you decrease costs and increase capacity. Primary storage takes place in main memory, which is very fast but has limited space and high volatility, and is very expensive. Secondary and tertiary storage media are usually optical or magnetic devices such as CD-ROMs, WORM disks, rewritable disks, magnetic disks, or magnetic tape. Secondary storage contains information used on a continual basis, and tertiary storage is used for backing up data and archiving inactive information. The traversal across these media is often transparent to the user, who sees all information in a seamless environment. The time it takes to access information located on these media is driven by factors such as your CPU speed, available RAM, data transfer and decompression speed, and disk changing time.

Fixed magnetic disks are well established in secondary storage and are desirable for high-performance access times and for their high storage capacity in large systems. Removable magnetic disks contain information that's used infrequently but accessible quickly once mounted. Magnetic tape drives store data off-line and are mounted when data is needed. Access time is slow because the data must be read sequentially. Magnetic tape drives are commonly used for data backup and archiving.

Due to the high data capacity of optical disks they are optimal for the storage of large text files, databases, and images and are particularly well suited for document-imaging systems and photo archiving. One way to maximize optical and magnetic characteristics is to store document images on an optical disk for efficiency and locate the index to the images on a fixed magnetic disk for database retrieval speed. Optical disk technology (CD-ROMs, WORM disks, rewritable disks) has several advantages over magnetic storage devices. These media are removable from the disk drive, are resistant to data corruption, and can store large amounts of information. The downside to optical devices is the access time required to retrieve the stored information.

CD-ROM technology was standardized by ISO 9960, which specifies the physical characteristics of the disks, how data is stored on the disks and the laser strength of the drives that read the disks. CD-ROMs can be read by almost any drive. Disks are read when a laser is focused on a track and the light detector registers the amount of light reflected back from the disk. If the reflection is similar to the laser beam's intensity, the value of zero is given. When the laser hits a pit on the disk, the light is scattered and the value assigned is one. This binary one/zero construct allows the data on the disk to be read, converted, and presented to the system user. Slow rotation speed, coupled with the tedious reading from pit to pit on the disk surface, means relatively slow access times.

WORM disks are standard 5¼" disks but utilize a variety of recording methods. The WORM (write once read many) disk takes the CD-ROM technology one step further by allowing the owner to write information to the disk. A common way information is written to a WORM disk is by laser heating, which causes a physical change to the disk that signifies that the disk may not be written to again. Once a WORM disk has been written to, the disk cannot be altered. This feature is useful for applications requiring audit trails and secure data archiving. Conversely, once the disk is filled, it must be replaced. If your data is constantly changing or being updated, WORM disks may not be for you.

Rewritable disks are a combination of magnetic and optical technology. Information is changed when a disk is heated and magnetized at a certain location. The information can be changed again only when the disk is heated and remagnetized. Data that is not of immediate need can be offloaded to this storage medium and accessed when needed, increasing data management efficiency. Rewritable disks are a good backup method because the disks can be written to repeatedly and removed from their drives for security. The standards for this technology are presently being developed by ISO and ANSI, so there is a multitude of disk sizes, recording methods, and drives.

Optical jukeboxes can corral from 5 to 100 optical disks, switch disks using a mechanical arm, and provide access to gigabits of data from a single location. When data is requested, the robot arm places the appropriate disk in the drive. Access time and bottlenecks depend on the number of users, number of drives and disks, RAM cache, and the mechanical arm itself. One way to improve performance is document staging, which stores files on the local workstation and deletes the file after it's used to free the space for another document. Documents can also be stored in a network cache space so they're available to all users on the network without taking up a lot of disk space. Multifunction jukeboxes are emerging on the marketplace that combine WORM and erasable disk technologies. This allows archival storage on secure, unchangeable disks and dynamic information storage on others. Again, a problem here is the lack of standards for WORM and rewritable media.

Comprehensive imaging standards are under development and an unresolved issue at this point. Groups such as CCITT, ISO, ANSI, and AIIM promote the development of standards in different areas with varying degrees success. There are standards for data compression, transmission, and communications. Hardware standards for WORM disks, rewritable disks, and disk drives are in committee under consideration. The concept of data compression has been worked to such a degree that several very sturdy standards have emerged. The Consultative Committee for International Telegraph and Telephone (CCITT) developed the Group 3 and Group 4 compression algorithms to enable fax transmission. The Group 3 standard led the way in 1980 with enough power to store mass amounts of documents. The Group 4 algorithm brought approximately a 30% increase in compression power when introduced. The compression of documents permits faster throughput, lower transmission costs, and the use of less storage space. Without data compression, the multimegabyte image files would drag network response time phenomenally. There is also a suite of standards regarding file formats. The file format is identified by the computer with the beginning bytes of an image file, called a file header. The file header describes information about the file, such as its size, resolution, and pixel representation. Some established file formats include GIF, TIFF, and the ever developing JPEG and MPEG.

The image server is used to retrieve and display electronic items in the imaging system. The server performs the functions of database searching, browsing items, displaying document images, and image manipulation. The server hardware and software are selected with a variety of factors, such as the type of files to be stored, the granularity of search capability desired, storage capacity, and budget.

Your image server hardware should be able to respond to requests for index information or images and interface via SCSI (scuzzy) drives linked to optical storage devices. Client-server applications with standard Ethernet connections give the flexibility to mix and match platform types, so an image server might be a UNIX box feeding high-resolution PCs or Macs. With a little bit of research you will uncover quite a bit of comparative literature for hardware at all levels of integration. You need an adequate CPU rate for acceptable throughput of data, enough RAM to hold multiple images, an image cache to stage documents, a good video graphics board, and, of course, a mouse.

The software for your system is the glue that connects the components. Given the operating system software (proprietary, DOS, or UNIX), the device driver software (to interface between peripherals and the CPU), and the utility software (word processing, forms, DTP, etc.), the true heart of the system is the database software. The quality of the database software determines how well you'll be able to retrieve the information you so carefully entered into the system. Therefore, the method for classifying and indexing your information should take precedence over your hardware selections. To put it bluntly, the system is only as good as your ability to get stuff back out of it!

The elements of bibliography, listing and finding items, remain central to the retrieval of electronic images. A tried-and-true tool for information retrieval is the traditional database management system (DBMS) that maintains hierarchical inverted files keyed to a specific set of attributes by which information can be retrieved. A relational DBMS permits retrieval of combinations of keyed items or access points. Databases retrieve information using Boolean, wild-card, and truncation search methods.

Another method for retrieving information is automatic indexing based on optical character recognition. The OCR software converts text areas to ASCII characters, which can be searched against in a full-text mode. OCR software can be combined with a computer thesaurus with assigned index terms to note conceptual relationships between broader, narrower, and related terms. Indexing can also be keyed to bar codes that are associated with each index entry. Developments in electronic indexing also include, among others, natural language inverted file structures and feature extraction.

Software on the high end of the scale performs pattern recognition, embedded OCR, RDBMS support, and fuzzy searching. Combinations of software and hardware architecture linked with document capture, storage, retrieval, and management abound. Systems that provide for the submission of natural language queries are breaking the mold of exclusion that many strict search methodologies maintain. Users are permitted to enter queries in a natural English-language phrase and retrieve pertinent information.

Media such as photographs, slides, diagrams, letters, and maps can't be converted into ASCII documents. Text is often inadequate to describe a graphical object. The image could be described textually without revealing its full meaning, relationships, and relevance. In these cases, the image must stand on its own and be viewed as the object it is, not as a secondhand description. You have to actually *see* the Mona Lisa's smile to wonder what it means. The notion that images can't "tell of themselves" presents opportunities for research in the area of access of visual objects. A bridge to self-describing images is software that provides text-based cataloging records coupled with sets of images to browse. There is some very promising work out of IBM Almaden concerning the use of visual objects to search for related visual items. Other research activities concerning aspects of the automation of image management include Project Athena at MIT, ImageNet at UC Berkeley, Project ICON at UT Austin, the NASA Electronic Library System (NELS), and many others. Investigation of visual access to visual objects, the automation of image description and retrieval, and the construction of algorithms and grammars to describe graphical objects are research activities that will make their way into the COTS image management products of tomorrow.

Some very good free software, obtainable from the public domain, performs the functions required of an enterprise-wide document management system. Public domain software of this nature can be identified with Internet finding tools like Gopher, Archie, and World Wide Web. One example of this type of software is known as WAIS (Wide Area Information Server). WAIS source code can be downloaded in various permutations from several locations around the world. With a single user interface WAIS provides access to local and remote datasets on heterogeneous platforms. It consists of three parts: the client, the server, and the protocol that connects them. When the user enters a natural-language query against a particular WAIS server (there are over 400), the request is sent out over a TCP/IP network wrapped in the ANSI Z39.50 protocol, which is a standard for the electronic transfer of information. The request is received at the specified server and the WAIS index routine searches the inverted files for matches to the query. The matches are assembled and ranked using heuristic algorithms based on percentages of occurrence and weighting for location in a record. This answer set is wrapped in the transfer protocol and shipped back over the TCP/IP network to the waiting client. The information returned contains the titles of the hits plus a ranked score that indicates how well the hits match the query that was submitted. This ranking, known as relevance feedback, assists the user in optimizing the search session. Any of the hits can be selected as search criteria for subsequent search sessions. Searches can also be saved for later use and updates. Users can create their own WAIS servers to classify and index internal information with access for a limited group or provide the server as a global WAIS resource by publishing the IP address in the directory of servers at quake.think.com.

There is a great deal of work occurring on WAIS technology in academic, government, and corporate circles. The NSF has funded a research effort (CNIDR) at the University of North Carolina to devise a standardized WAIS platform. Research at NASA is focusing on the development of a WAIS extended client to add heterogeneous metadata attributes and sophisticated viewers to the information server technology. MCC recently released friendly graphical interfaces for WAIS connectivity through its EINet (Enterprise Integration Network). Contributions from academia include a Hypercard version of WAIS, a PC version of WAIS, and modifications to the search engine to include Boolean, wild-card, and pattern matching for those diehards who must have them.

Another very interesting piece of public domain software is known as XMosaic. XMosaic is a hypertext front end to the World Wide Web (WWW) out of Cern, Switzerland. It's an X-Windows-based interface that has embedded hypertext links that connect the user to servers around the world. It retrieves the requested information, pulls it across the net, and presents it to the user in real time. It supports still graphics, sound, video, animation and text. The hypertext files for WWW are created using a format known as HTML, Hypertext Markup Language. Development of hypertext datasets will grow with the further development and refinement of this technology.

To summarize, document-imaging systems provide substantial advantages over the traditional paper-based information management systems. Information can be efficiently stored on high-density storage media that are easy to access by one or many people. The information can be easily retrieved with various types of search engines and delivered quickly and accurately to the requester. Information management systems can also incorporate other work applications, such as workforms or word processing functions, to increase output and efficiency.

To successfully evaluate and select an electronic management system, detailed research about your existing organization must be performed to achieve maximum benefits. Use conservative estimates as you plan and stick with as many open standards as you can. The imaging industry continues to mature, and as it does, costs will keep dropping and performance will go up. Digital enterprise-wide information management will eventually be the de facto standard for the workplace.

REFERENCES

Knack, C.J. "Paperless Office Still a Myth in the Nineties." *Office.* v117. n4. p.25. April, 1993.

Knack, C.J. "The Paperless Office (State of the Art)." *Byte.* v16. n4. p.156. April, 1991. AIIM. *Information and Image Management, the State of the Industry.* New York, AIIM, 1987.

Wolk, Sue. "AIIM Takes CAT Scan of the Industry--Special Report of Imaging Industry." *Government Computer News.* Sept. 14, 1992.

Wallace, Andy. "Justifying the Image." *Datamation.* v36. n8. p.82. 1990.

Susan Cisco
Suite 1204
2901 Barton Skyway
Austin, Texas 78746
(512) 328-0127
CompuServe 73150.242

11. INDEXING DOCUMENTS FOR IMAGING SYSTEMS

The indexing scheme is the most important component of a document imaging system and is essential to the efficient management of information in a system. Yet most vendor literature and the popular press make little mention of indexing as it relates to imaging systems except to acknowledge that the process requires "manual" effort.

Definitions

- **Indexing parameters** denote categories of information by which documents will be indexed for subsequent retrieval. They correspond to fields in database records and are delineated for an application as a whole.
- **Indexing values** are the characters, words, or phrases associated with specific documents in a manner determined by the indexing parameters.

Design of Indexing Schemes

The design of a good document indexing scheme is often a complex task requiring analysis of the ways in which documents will be requested and definition of indexing parameters according to database criteria. If a document is not indexed by a given parameter, it cannot be retrieved by that parameter. Thus, determination of relevant indexing parameters needs to be done long before the imaging system is brought in-house. This step requires conceptualizing the meaning of the documents and selecting parameters by which the documents will be requested.

Something that has to be taken into account when developing indexing schemes for imaging systems, especially in large networked systems, is identifying retrieval needs for those in the organization who are outside the immediate user group. These users may make very different use of the information than the main user group and can be expected to request the document by different parameters.

In addition, very often it is not necessary for users of document imaging systems to actually view a record. Rather, it is information from the document that is needed to satisfy the request. Keeping this in mind, designers of indexing schemes for document imaging systems should include those items of information in the indexing scheme that provide answers to the request without the user having to view the document. To accomplish this, the essential pieces of information for given document categories need to be incorporated into the indexing data.

When to Index Documents

When converting hard-copy documents to optical disk, there are two approaches for capturing index values: (1) scan the documents, then index them, or (2) index the documents, then scan them. When documents are scanned first, they are scanned in batches and the digitized images are held in buffer storage (typically, magnetic disk). The document images are displayed on high-resolution monitors/workstations, which not only permit entry of the indexing values, but can also allow simultaneous quality control to be made of every image. The principal drawback of this method is the cost of the high-resolution monitors.

With the second method, the first step is indexing batches of documents using standard data entry techniques and personal computers or conventional data entry terminals. Double-entry indexing (first entry and verification) can be done using different operators. Header sheets may be printed and inserted in the document batches at appropriate places for subsequent control purposes. The main drawback of this approach is the need for a separate quality control process.

The decision to scan first or index first depends upon the unique requirements of each organization. For example, at the United States Automobile Association (USAA) in San Antonio, indexing values are entered prior to scanning. This speeds up processing by allowing the analyst to deal with exceptional situations, such as payments that should be refused and returned, original documents that need to be returned, or forms that need to be filled out. Because the analyst makes critical decisions before scanning, the operation is more efficient than if every document were scanned prior to dealing with exceptions.

Automatic Indexing

Because indexing can represent over 50% of the total document entry in an imaging system, techniques to accelerate the process are being explored and utilized. These include reading a bar code on the document, a pattern in the image, and mark sense codes. Indexing values also can be derived by means of optical character recognition (OCR) and using existing databases for extracting and/or downloading index data.

BAR CODES

Bar codes work like Morse code except that instead of encoding data in dots and dashes, bar codes use bars and spaces of different widths. While its most widespread application is the simple identification of document type, any information, alpha or numeric, can be bar-coded, written, and read back with low error rates.

PATTERN RECOGNITION

Software has been developed that analyzes images of electronic documents by various methods, including neural networks. These products can be "trained" to respond to the same kind of image patterns that enable people to recognize forms at a glance. The system is trained by giving it as many examples of each kind of form one wishes it to recognize. During the training process, particular areas of a form may be registered, such as a box containing characters that must be recognized. After training, when presented with an image of a form, the system can identify the name of that form. Pattern recognition works even when the form has been filled out and is frequently used in high-volume transaction processing.

MARK SENSE CODES

Mark sense codes are similar to the bubbles filled in on standardized multiple-choice tests or reader response cards in magazines. The process of filling in the bubbles actually digitizes the responses. A scanner passes over the marks and reads them automatically into a computer. Mark sense codes can be applied to indexing when an organization sends a form to a customer who fills it out and returns it.

OPTICAL CHARACTER RECOGNITION (OCR)

OCR is a technology that converts an electronic picture of a document into a form that text-based applications, such as word processors, spreadsheets, and databases, can handle. Technically, OCR takes a picture of a character and converts it into an ASCII character. Although different systems specialize in font and hand-print recognition, recognizing cursive handwriting is still difficult.

EXISTING DATABASES

Many organizations wisely avoid rekeying indexing values by importing the necessary data from existing databases. Another advantage of this approach is that existing data (at least, theoretically) already has been proofread and corrected.

Cost of Indexing Documents

Different people calculate indexing cost in different ways. For example, David B. Black presents a methodology for calculating indexing costs in his book *Document Capture for Document Imaging Systems.* To calculate the cost of indexing and quality checking, take the capital costs, add labor rate, and divide by throughput to get a cost per document.

Dr. William Saffady also presents a methodology for calculating indexing costs in an article entitled "Document Indexing in CAR and Optical Filing Systems (*Micrographics and Optical Storage Equipment Review* 13: 97-116, 1988). He divides indexing labor costs into two groups: (1) document analysis costs associated with the selection of index values for specific parameters, and (2) data entry costs associated with conversion of the selection index values to machine-readable form. Of the two groups, document analysis costs are usually significantly greater than their data entry counterparts.

Document conversion services typically charge by the project because indexing schemes vary in difficulty. In a typical manual indexing operation, the cost of having an indexer read the entire text of a document to identify keywords is much higher than identification of more obvious index values such as "date of correspondence." Prices quoted on a particular project are calculated based on these differences.

Standards

One promising alternative for capturing indexing data is standardized mark-up languages that describe a document's content when created. This idea has been given a boost by the government's Computer-Aided Acquisition and Logistics Support initiative (CALS), which requires SGML (Standard Generalized Markup Language), an International Standards Organization standard. Once index values are tagged in SGML, they can be searched by the database.

The Association for Information and Image Management (AIIM) also is active in setting indexing standards for document imaging; (1) ANSI/AIIM MS55, Identification and Indexing of Page Components (Zones) for Automated Processing in an EIM Environment and (2) ANSI/AIIM MS56, Index Fields for Processing and Retrieval of Documents in an EIM System.

VIII. TRAINING

Unfortunately, many libraries believe that they can't afford training time — they need people working right now. This idea was unrealistic in the past, and now as we move toward the electronic library, it is a fantasy. The next chapter by Maggie Gonzalez is about training. Maggie's job at the Engineering Library is to train our student and clerical workers. Part of this includes training them to use our various electronic tools. This is important because often in the evening and weekends they are the only library staff in the library. They must be able to show freshman international students, senior faculty, and the local body shop man how to find information — how to navigate electronically. A daunting task.

Maggie Gonzalez
Library Assistant III
Engineering Library
The General Libraries
The University of Texas at Austin
LLMAG@utxdp.dp.utexas.edu

12. GROUND ZERO: TRAINING STAFF

The basic idea behind training, electronic or any other type, is the concept of repetition. The more ways you can approach a task the better. I have also found that the more senses you can utilize or reach, the greater the retention. I usually try to use sight, hearing, and touch. The trainer's initial approach should be to touch on all topics with the hope of minimal retention. That is, you merely broach all topics and ask the trainee to remember certain specific portions of information, such as how to begin. Another important aspect is that trainees become familiar with their surroundings--usually this is done on the first day. They are in a new environment and are being bombarded with all kinds of new stimuli, and in most cases they feel uncomfortable and under some stress. The most you can expect anyone to remember, under those circumstances, has to be minimal.

The next important aspect is to give the new staff an idea of what the long- and short-range expectations are for every task, including familiarity with electronic information and how to retrieve it. It is important that they feel comfortable in their surroundings and know where to go to find things, whether that is a physical place or an individual. At this point, you need to be able to break down each critical or important task into no more than 10 or 11 basic steps. Each trainee should be given a packet that consists of policies and written procedures.

The new staff members should search through the training packet, locate the pertinent steps for each task, and write them up in a short 1, 2, 3 format. I have observed that the actual job of locating or hunting down information and producing a written document helps them retain the procedures to be followed. Performing this task utilizes the senses of sight and touch. Again, I reiterate that the more senses you can reach (or tap into) the more you can count on having the information become part of their basic foundation of knowledge.

Another aspect of training that I find to be critical is the new staff members need to feel that they have not been left totally to fend for themselves. It is usually a good idea to designate an individual as a mentor or work buddy for each new staff member. The mentor serves as a reference source when the new member doesn't remember something, has to meet an entirely new sitution, or feels uncomfortable about doing a task. The mentor system works well for many aspects of training your new staff, providing not only a reference source, but also someone to observe them actually doing the various tasks before they undertake them on their own. The one thing that the trainees should be assured of, from the first day of work, is that any new task will be done with the assistance of one of the more experienced staff members or supervisors. The task of this staff member is first to inquire what the new staff member knows about that particular job.

The answer to that first question tells the supervisor (or experienced staff member) where to begin in helping the newer staff member complete and/or start the job. It is beneficial for the new staff members to have someone right on hand to ask questions of, as well as someone to remind them that they have missed a step. This gives the trainees a chance to see what they really remember and gives the supervisor some idea of what information has already been absorbed or where problems may arise. This is also a good indicator of how well the new staff members are progressing with the training information they were initially given.

One of the things I find most useful is to remember that training does not stop after the first, second, or fourth day. New staff members have to feel that they receive follow-up and feedback during the initial period of orientation. Orientation is not something you can contain in a set period of time that is the same for everyone. Some people grasp and retain information more quickly than others, so you have to tailor an orientation and training period to the individual. By asking my new staff to read and ask questions about the training information, I can pinpoint where they may be having trouble grasping concepts or procedures. This also enables me to clarify information that they think they are having problems with.

Second, I ask my new staff to put the six most important pieces of information on a set of 3-by-5 cards (not to exceed two cards); it is preferable to try and put it all on one card using the back and front to record information. The card acts as a ready reference tool and also gives them an indication of what they are expected to know backwards and forwards on a daily basis.

The third, and by no means the least important training technique, is quizzing your staff periodically. You can do this in a group setting, or on an individual basis.*

*This is good for quality control as well as reminding the staff what good service means.

The group setting helps both you and your staff. It allows you to listen to the variety of answers and their interpretations. Having a group meeting, in a timely fashion, allows for a greater likelihood that there will be open discussion. The meeting allows the staff to discuss problems or suggestions, as well as giving the supervisor the opportunity to talk about changes in procedures or new and upcoming policies and/or training. The act of quizzing reemphasizes the importance of knowing basic information and also makes the staff aware that it is not just information they need to know where to find, but that there is truly a purpose and they are expected to know it. The repetition of basic information is worthwhile simply to reinforce its importance. Quizzing an individual allows you to see just how quickly the staff member can bring the particular information to mind if asked. The drawback to meeting with staff members one-on-one is that it is an awkward difficult setting for imparting new information or new training procedures, mainly because you have to say the same thing over and over.

One of the library's newest approaches to training has been to videotape basic job tasks. I have found this videotape to be very useful as a supplement to a verbal presentation. I discovered I had the best results when I used the videotape to reinforce training I had already done. When the video was used as an introduction it was sometimes confusing or disregarded as a source of information altogether. In its short history with us, I have found videotape to be a worthwhile tool. Our long-range ideas are to use a Hypercard program of some sort to assist in instruction and possibly in evaluating. This would allow for more individual training and could be repeated as needed.

In electronic searching (Internet, CD-ROMs, LANs, OPACs) the most important aspect is that your staff know what the system should look like and how it should act so that they can be aware of when it is not working. At the very least, staff must know how to get each electronic system back to the entry screen, or to a familiar level at which they can help the user continue or start again. Of course, this can be accomplished only through using the computer itself. Staff need to memorize a short procedure for operating the computer. You must decide what level of intricacies you want each employee to know. But most of all, all employees must be able to get the computer back to the main screen. They must be able to evaluate who to call for more complex help, and they must be able to determine when the equipment is broken or not functioning..

In short, training is an ongoing practice in order to be sure your staff is always alert and informed on current policies and procedures. Your staff is only as good as your ongoing training and evaluation are, and all this requires time.

IX. MARKETING

Let's face marketing issue squarely: marketing is like taxes—always with us — and now more than ever librarians need to get the resources they need, justify what they do, and explain why their activities are neither trivial nor inexpensive.

The three articles that follow cover many aspects of how librarians engage in marketing. The first, "Bringing Home the Bacon," is by an academic librarian, and the second, "From Librarian to Cybrarian" is by two corporate librarians who discuss marketing with a different spin and with a different focus. However, both articles make the point that the meek get nothing in this world. The last article, "Reach Out Electronically," also by an academic librarian, offers some specific advice on delivering service outside the library, a concept that really ties this whole book together.

Dennis Trombatore
Geology Librarian
The General Libraries
The University of Texas at Austin
LLDRT@utxdp.dp.utexas.edu.

13. BRINGING HOME THE BACON: AUTOMATING LIBRARY SERVICES IN A MARKETING CONTEXT

Even without any books or journals at all in your library (or only books and journals, and no computers), you have to continuously achieve your institutional goal: providing information services to your primary clientele in support of your organization's mission. Especially in today's world of wrenching changes in organizations and society, each and every component of an enterprise must be aware of the constant shifting of institutional needs and expectations. Moreover, all cost center managers must always ask themselves whether the work they do every day is:

- appropriate work for their organization
- cost effective, timely, and more efficient than last year
- contributing measurably to the product's value or excellence
- recognized in the organization for these attributes

This chapter will be primarily about the last item, and no matter what environment a library operates in, the fundamental principles of marketing apply.

You can see the library or information center as a kind of golden goose. If your constituency is allowed to take for granted what you provide, complacency (yours and theirs) sets in, and the temptation for your umbrella organization to serve you up on a platter will eventually be irresistible.

What are the key concepts here? They are: constituency, complacency, and cooperation. Every library is part of an institutional ecosystem. To survive and to achieve your goals you must know where you are on the food chain. You do this by understanding and employing the fundamental concepts of marketing.

Every group of people in an organization, particularly those with definable tasks, must learn to see themselves in this marketing context: as elements in a complex web of relationships that both define what is possible in organizational life and determine the definition of success and failure.

In the first two editions of his groundbreaking textbook Marketing for Nonprofit Organizations, (Prentice-Hall, 1975, 1982) Philip Kotler outlines the basic principles and practices of marketing in a not-for-profit context. This text is almost required reading for library managers who expect to survive in this period of dislocation and rapid change. A subsequent, more advanced text by Kotler, *Strategic Marketing for Nonprofit Organizations* (Prentice-Hall, 1987), carries these basic principles into practice.

Kotler's work centers on several basic marketing fundamentals that he adapts for those whose work with clients is not primarily for monetary gain, or those who, by analogy, work inside a larger organization or bureaucracy — whether nonprofit or for-profit.

Crucial is the understanding that successful marketing relies on shrewd and accurate assessment of ongoing market relations. You must be able to answer the following questions.

- What does your organization value?
- Is your organization open or closed? Growing or surviving? Freewheeling or hierarchical? Innovative or conservative?
- How is that value quantified, described, and exchanged?
- What are the reward structures of your organization? Is success measured in physical space, travel, equipment, staff support, or some other extra that denotes the importance of your contribution?
- How are these rewards dispensed, and by whom?
- What have others done that has been rewarded?
- Which parts of your organization are "target markets" for the values and services you provide?
- Is there fair exchange of real value among the various units?
- For instance, does purchasing know you can provide vendor information?
- Or does the physical plant staff know you can provide product evaluations?
   *What organizational components have never requested assistance? Do you know why?

- What kind of support do you get in return from your steady customers?
- How many such target markets are there in your organization or among its clients for library services, and how are they similar or different?
- Does your organization have a records management plan?
- Are there remote sites that need regular attention from the home office?
- Do you have regular contact and working relations with someone in facilities, technical support, fiscal and personnel services, field operations, marketing, R&D, or any other divisions that might have need for information services?
- Which parts of the organization see the library as one of their "target markets" and how are relations with them structured? Is there fair exchange of real value between the library and these units?
- What is the library's relationship with computer services or purchasing?   *How do physical plant needs get resolved?
- Is the library getting good value from these exchanges, or is it a cash cow for other cost centers? It is essential to cut through appearances to an understanding of (1) what is of meaningful, functional significance to your organization, (2) how properly to describe these values as missions or goals, and (3) whether or not what the library provides is a genuine match for those real values.
- What means you use to provide these services is important only in terms of outcomes:
  o Is the service fast enough?
  o Is it accurate enough?
  o Is it appropriately matched with your client's capabilities?

Increasingly, this means providing information in an automated or digital environment, but format is subsidiary to results.

It is a mistake to assume that marketing is just another term for advertising or cynical prevarication — mere packaging, in short. While packaging is a component of marketing, a realistic marketing plan is not like an alchemist's conjuring or a snake-oil salesman's pitch. Ethical marketing is based on the reality that a successful strategy must have good consequences. A marketing plan must be an honest one if the library is going to hold the trust and confidence of its target markets and succeed with them.

The practical meaning of this is that the designer of a successful marketing plan must (1) identifiy the real values of the organization and how those values are described and measured, (2) determine what the web of producer/client relations is and where the library fits best, and (3) work to ensure that the library actually accomplishes what the plan requires.

That is, either the library is doing what needs to be done and must communicate that properly (to the right people, at the right time, in the right way), or the library must adapt to its target market, find new target markets to serve, or if all else fails, alter the entire structure of the organization to support the library's needs. In any case, whatever changes are needed, proper communication is a key element. Communication strategy includes:

- Who to communicate with
- When and how to accomplish this communication
- Packaging and feedback

Clearly, the advertising and packaging components of marketing, while significant, are the last and in some sense the easiest pieces of the puzzle.

A Case Study

As an example of technology-driven marketing in an electronic environment, the librarian of a medical center might decide that CD-ROM technology is now mature enough, with a wide enough range of specifically useful products and some stability and standardization, that it could win over her fundamentally conservative organization. This organization's focus is health care, but its organizational structure is more typically administrative, hierarchical, and accounting oriented.

Of primary concern to these managers are floor space and per-square-foot cost, and it is clear that automation efforts which return space and efficiency in good ratio to price will be favorably received. The librarian has already seen that the medical records division has received approval to automate, with the expectation of eventually making on-line patient charting a reality, and that the purchasing department has CD-ROM catalogs from several major dealers for equipment procurement. These efforts are not in competition with information the library wants to make available, but they do demonstrate the viability of the concept.

The librarian gathers information about hardware needs and hardware options that are also practical for her organization. She determines which products would appeal to the broadest client base and how users would be likely to interfere with each other in terms of frequency of use, depth of need, training requirements, etc. This helps her establish quantitatively the extent of resources — hardware, software, information products, and, from these, funding and space — which will support a spectrum of offerings from minimal to generous. This makes choices easier later.

During her three years at this facility, the librarian has developed good working relations with the computer center staff, helping them find product evaluations and supporting their general information needs. She is confident of their support and good advice. On the other hand, the director of telephone and communication services is obstructive and poorly informed. Thus her original plan to attempt a larger-scale network will have to wait on smaller successes. She will focus on one or more stand-alone workstations as a way to begin the electronic chapter of her library's existence.

She has determined that floor space and furniture needs can be met without outside assistance, at least in the start-up phase. She knows where several necessary pieces of furniture are that are about to be upgraded and can be secured as hand-me-downs. She has also selected materials to withdraw and has determined that she can rearrange space to make an attractive workstation area in only a day or two. Open space draws unwanted attention in this facility, however, so this will not be executed until the last minute. The existing space arrangement will serve as a placeholder until the proper moment. Power supplies are adequate, and when the time comes, the location is accessible for cable and/or data lines.

The librarian's obvious target market is physicians, so she designs the components and products to provide them with the shortest path to their goals. For instance, this requires a fast, high-quality printer. These primary clients won't sit still for downloading and doodling with disks. Nevertheless, there are many other potential beneficiaries, and she prioritizes their needs based on several factors, including product availability and cost, size of user population and their influence on decision making, and appropriate fit with the primary goal.

Some of the ancillary users are physicians' staffs and clerical assistants, nurses, pharmacy staff, a small research cadre, EMS personnel, patient advocates (this facility is not open to patients), and the organization's public relations and marketing coordinator.

The range of users creates a potential problem, because while the staff physicians are primarily users of DOS-based machines, Apple products are beginning to make inroads with the residents and other potential users. Additionally, the utility of downloading information for later reuse will require that the librarian be prepared to accomplish both downloading and file transfer/exchange procedures (FTP) as well as quality print production. She determines that the resources are available to supply these needs, provided she herself learns the necessary skills or delegates the task to a staffer who is willing and readily available during office hours.

Finally, the librarian investigates the products and various hidden costs they may invoke — licensing agreements, headaches about registered users, increased demands for new or difficult-to-provide materials and services, maintenance, upgrades, etc. She is now ready to develop her strategy, write her proposal, and present it to the appropriate people in an appropriate forum.

This librarian is fully prepared. She has staked out her target markets, charted the opportunities and challenges, obtained all the required information, played out the consequences of getting what she is asking for, and lined up supporters. She is now ready to implement her marketing plan. Her chances of success are greatly improved because surprises are unlikely, but if the request is denied, she has all the puzzle pieces ready to reorganize and try again.

Analysis and Issues

A marketing plan is like a jigsaw puzzle. First you look at the big picture. Then you recapitulate it by reassembling bits and pieces to match: the framework, the major elements, the piece you have in your hand, etc. One big difference is that a jigsaw puzzle is an end in itself. Once the last piece drops in, the task is complete.

The marketing plan, however, is a tool, and the next big hurdle is to move from analysis and planning to implementation and feedback. Getting bogged down with the endless task of perfecting your marketing plan is *not* the goal; the goal is to ensure that your library is an efficient, vital contributor to your organization's products and services.

Once a workable program is outlined, it must be put into practice, evaluated, and then "morphed" — adapted to fit the inevitable changes in the big picture. This is not a process to be accomplished in two hours a week or for the purpose of generating an edifying report. This is a process for getting your head straight about what matters in your organization and what doesn't. It is also a framework for action that you as the library manager will carry into every deliberation, project, and encounter and will work to ensure that staff understand and implement.

A librarian must be prepared to measure success with the ruler his or her organization uses. The library exists to serve the specific information needs of some certain clientele, and it is the specific, identifiable values of those clients that are the measuring stick of success. It matters little if the library engages in a variety of good works if those works are of no perceptible benefit to the organization as a whole. This means that the library must do appropriate things and describe them in a meaningful way.

This may unsettle librarians who have their own professional aspirations and values to uphold, or who wish to be left alone to do what they believe is appropriate, but if the librarian's values are the library's values, and if those values are mismatched with those of the organization, then neither the library nor the librarian is likely to be successful. In such a case, a basic marketing plan would call for the librarian to adapt, change the client base, change the organization, or leave. This is particularly true since many corporate or special libraries are likely to be one-professional (or one-person) operations.

In larger library structures, more room exists for compromise and development of individual librarian's differences, or at least this has been true in the past. If the library as a whole is successful, some portion of its staff or other resources may be allowed to be lavished on special activities or larger goals for the general good. Such activities might include special collections, outreach or community consortium activities, or individual research and publication. All these activities advance the profile and reputation of the organization, but they are not, in the strict sense, essential. Ultimately, libraries must first provide information services for their institutional clients, who provide funding for that purpose first and foremost.

If the fit is poor, the library is more likely to fail than the organization, although both will suffer. The organization will have to fund information services in two ways — one unsuccessful, formal way called a library, and another, perhaps underground, way that works but is described as something else. This is costly and wasteful. The umbrella organization will find some way to obtain the information services that it values, whether it supports the library or not; the library, on the other hand, *must* have the support of its umbrella organization.

Thus, the *independence* of the library is determined by the *interdependence* of the umbrella organization's components with the services and information the library provides. These relationships are dynamic, and as they unfold, the library must be prepared to evolve. Today the pressure to evolve or to go extinct is greater than ever.

For the past two decades, the major evolutionary thrust in libraries has been the digitization, compression, and transmission of information. While there has been a lot of hollow posturing about the ramifications of these technology developments, a genuine revolution has occurred in libraries and in the institutions they serve. That revolution is leading to a shakeout, and after some (significant) dislocation, there will be a consolidation of gains and changes in publishing, in information storage and delivery, in the expectations placed on libraries, and on the profession of librarianship.

Staying afloat and demonstrating success during these changes will require the ability to discern (paraphrasing CNN's Ted Turner) when to lead, when to follow, and when to get out of the way. Sometimes the library will be in a position to lead the way to new information technologies or to signal danger when bad ideas are proposed. In such situations the librarian must be prepared to *use* technology to *sell* technology or, conversely, use his or her skills to raise awareness of alternatives.

At other times, technology will be imposed, and the librarian must be prepared to follow that development with the ice-breaking activity that shows the path to full utilization of the new systems. Occasionally, bad institutional technology decisions are inevitable, and the librarian must be prepared to quickly assess the failure potential of such decisions and get out of the way of the fallout, thus protecting the integrity of library services and operations.

This is consistent with the well-thought-out marketing plan — the library, properly perceived as the switching center or hub of certain institutional information services, takes an active role in developing, exploring, and promoting the best new systems and capabilities. It is important to conceive of this not just within the library, but in order to fully link and open the library to target markets within the organization. In this way, the library adds value to the information provided by making it easier and quicker to get and offering it more tailored for reuse than anyone else can. This ultimatley adds value to the organization's products and services.

Up until now, the reason libraries existed at all was the result of the relative transcendence of a technology — printing or writing on (virtually) two-dimensional sheets of cellulose. The fact that such artifacts exist, persist, and contain meaningful information for reuse makes possible the gathering, organization, and dissemination that is still a librarian's business. Conceptually, the transcendence of that paper technology across time and cultures is at an end, and even though library processes continue, what this implies for the fundamental function of libraries must be considered by every librarian.

Theodore Levitt suggested in his classic paper on marketing principles "Marketing Myopia" (*Harvard Business Review* 38, July-Aug 1960: pp. 45-56) that many "mature" industries like railroads and steel sowed the seeds of their own destruction by failing to maintain a vision of what their true business interests were. The native tendencies of bureaucracies and organizations, once established, to turn their efforts toward self-preservation and aggrandizement may be fundamental to this weakness.

Libraries in our society are now "mature" industries, and the technology base they are built on has become the target of competition and revitalization. The dominance of paper and all its attendant technologies is in question. Essentially, the unified concept of a library (a *collection* of materials and the services provided *from* it) is evolving under a variety of environmental pressures into a family of more specialized organizations with variable shapes — collections and services are still fundamental notions, but the focus is shifting to the information niche itself, and the librarian's task is to exploit *all* the relevant technologies to provide a good fit within the niche (i.e. market) in which they find themselves.

Holding these concepts firmly in mind and using them creatively and flexibly to demonstrate accepted institutional values makes the librarian a unique asset to any organization — someone inside looking out for the best interests of the organization as a whole, someone who ideally helps to define and advance those interests by bringing every useful information technology to bear on whatever goal is central to the enterprise.

The real fun of being a successful librarian is the charge that accompanies closing the connection in the marketing feedback loop: when each part of the organization understands the library's special contribution to its particular mission, and when the library fulfills those expectations consistently and appropriately. In today's change-driven environment, the librarian must constantly raise the level of the dialogue.

Barbara Denton
barbara_denton@sematech.org
Marilyn Redmond
marilyn_redmond@sematech.org
SEMATECH
Austin, Tx.

14. FROM LIBRARIAN TO CYBRARIAN: REINVENTING OUR PROFESSION

A corporation that is serious about its information needs may contemplate having . . . a network of cybrarians (i.e. librarians able to navigate in 'cyberspace'), strategically located throughout the company.

Michel Bauwens, "Cybrarians' Manifesto"
PACS-L discussion list, 4/20/93

A fundamental change is occurring in the way our library customers obtain and use information. As new information tools emerge, our customers have more and more alternatives to waiting for a busy librarian to provide traditional library services. Our customers can find answers by posting a question on an Internet discussion list or by running a quick search on whatever database is available at their desktop. Why wait for a librarian to do a literature search?

The days when our skills as information intermediaries made us indispensable are disappearing. Our companies need us more as leaders; they need our vision of the possibilities of emerging information tools and our ability to transform our companies into effective users of those tools.

The Sematech librarians are developing a vision and strategic plan for the next five years. The authors are leading this process, drawing on the ideas and experience of our colleagues, our customers, and our suppliers. This paper describes the challenges facing corporate libraries, our vision of how SEMATECH will adapt to meet those challenges, several approaches that you as a library manager can take to develop and implement your own version of this vision, and the lessons we are learning along the way.

Sematech is a consortium of eleven semiconductor manufacturers and is based in Austin, Texas. The SEMATECH Library staff consists of three librarians and two part-time MLIS student interns, and supports about a thousand customers. Two librarians work in other departments as "cybrarians," that is, they focus on that department's information needs.

Five more librarians and another MLIS student intern work at Sematech. One manages Strategic Information Services, which includes the Library and the Records Management and Archives group. Another manages Records Management and Archives, and an MLIS student intern works in that group. A third librarian manages the document writing and editing department in the Technology Transfer division, and a fourth indexes our Technology Transfer documents and maintains the database containing their abstracts. The fifth works in the Total Quality division, teaching employees to write performance plans and quality measures.

The Challenges That Face Us

FROM MANAGEMENT

Like everyone else in this tight economy, corporate librarians are challenged to fulfill their mission with limited resources. As demands on our time and budget increase, it becomes crucial to analyze costs and benefits of every product and service we offer and eliminate anything that is not worth the purchase price or the staff time. Every minute, every dollar, and every skill available to us must be focused on the activities that are critical to our mission.

We are not alone in this process analysis. As other areas in our organizations review their operations, we may be asked to accept new responsibilities. It is essential to avoid letting our zeal to prove that librarians can do anything make us accept tasks that are unrelated to our mission.

FROM OUR CUSTOMERS

Many customers seem to believe not only the negative stereotype of the forbidding librarian, but also the positive stereotype that libraries are wonderful for their own sake. Both are inaccurate and potentially damaging to the effectiveness of the corporate library. Compounding this problem, customers adjust their expectations to whatever level of service their own library offers, no matter how minimal. As a result, every library customer survey seems to generate extremely positive evaluations, but few tangible indicators of success.

If corporate libraries and librarians are perceived merely as "nice to have around," we are sure to disappear in the next round of budget cuts. It is essential that we raise our customers' expectations and rise to the challenge of meeting them. We must set milestones and measurable criteria for our success, ensure that we produce concrete results, and seek recognition for our accomplishments.

Corporate librarians are responsible for meeting all of our customers' information needs, whether they ask us to do the research and analyze the results; prefer to do their research themselves, relying on us only to facilitate access to information tools; or they never use the library.

Although corporate librarians often claim to support the entire company, a large number of our potential customers do not use our services. To find out how to fulfill those unmet information needs, we should interview noncustomers whenever possible. We can ask how they obtain and use information and what we could do to provide it. Are they unaware of our services? Are our services not accessible enough? Do we lack a service they need?

It seems that most people will not go more than twenty feet to get information, so we must be accessible within those twenty feet. We must either find a way to be physically nearby when the question occurs to the customer, or to be virtually nearby via phone, fax, E-mail, or an icon on the desktop computer. An increasingly information-literate number of our customers challenge us to support their needs for database and local library access, to stay ahead of them on the learning curve, and to select and provide the best of a wealth of new information resources.

FROM OUR PROFESSION

We must prove that we can add real value to our results, not simply serve as an intermediary between a customer and the arcane search language of a database. We have the skills to refine raw data into useful knowledge, but often do not take the time. It is our responsibility to find creative ways to accomplish routine tasks, freeing us to put our best efforts into the most important work.

As corporate librarians, we continually market our key services to all levels — company-wide, to departments, to project teams, and to individuals. Successful marketing increases demand for our services, forcing us to find ways to handle a growing workload without letting the quality of service suffer. How can we add value if we can't keep up with demand?

If we can meet all of these challenges, we will fulfill the spirit of our mission statement and make a real contribution to the success of our company.

The Vision

Michel Bauwens's article "Cybrarians' Manifesto" appeared on PACS-L just in time to have a significant impact on our discussion of our vision. Bauwens invented the term "cybrarian" to describe the new breed of librarians who are comfortable with electronic information resources, from commercial databases to the Internet, and who do not necessarily work in a room full of books.

Bauwens envisions a new corporate information model consisting of a network of cybrarians, each focusing on the needs of a small group of internal customers. Cybrarians will combine expertise in information resources with specialized expertise in their group's subject area, improving the quality of their reference interviews and their research results. They will have fewer projects, so will be able to put more time into each one.

Corporate librarians will still exist but they will adapt to a new role. They will support the network of cybrarians by facilitating communication and cooperation among them, negotiating with external information suppliers, and identifying emerging information technologies. The corporate library will continue to support the information needs of groups without cybrarians and individuals' needs for information on general topics such as management and employee development. To reduce the cost in dollars and staff time of maintaining a print collection, the librarians will purchase materials based on the concept of "just in time" rather than "just in case."

Bauwens' vision fit in very well with our Sematech vision. We have experimented with several aspects of this idea recently with positive results.

IMPLEMENTING THE VISION

Reinventing the way your company obtains and uses information may take several years to accomplish. At Sematech, we have used five approaches:

- Describe and rank library functions
- Review work processes for each function
- Reinvent or eliminate library functions
- Develop a network of power information users
- Develop a network of cybrarians

What do you do?

Can you explain to your CEO (or your mother) what you do for a living? Do you know how you spend your time? Is 80% of your time and your budget being spent on the most important 20% of your tasks? If you were faced with staff or budget cuts, what functions would you eliminate? What would be the effect on your mission?

Answer these questions by listing your services. Describe each one in a few words without jargon and rank them in order of importance to your mission. How much does each one cost? How much staff time does each one take?

At Sematech, we did this step in June 1992 as part of a benchmarking study. The one-page chart we developed at the time has been invaluable, guiding decisions on marketing, new services, service cuts, and setting priorities when we are swamped.

Pick the Low-hanging Fruit

Review the work flow in every function and look for ways to improve the process. Look for awkward or unnecessary steps, routines that can be automated, human or bureaucratic obstacles, and ways to improve service with little additional cost or time.

At Sematech, we did this in a series of 45-minute process review sessions over a ten-month period, each led by the person responsible for the function being reviewed. We each found that as we prepared our presentations, several improvements became immediately obvious. Several more came out of the presentation and brainstorming session.

These incremental process improvements had an immediate positive effect. Many improvements took little time or money to implement and had comparatively dramatic results.

However, even after reviewing all our services, we found that we still had not gained enough time to keep up with the growth in demand for our services, much less invest more time in adding value to our output. A more drastic approach was needed.

Reinvent Every Function

Take a hard look at every library function to determine whether it can be eliminated, reinvented, or outsourced. Ask:

- Is it critical to achieving our mission?
- Why are we doing this? Is it "just in case" or "just in time"?
- Are we duplicating work that is being done elsewhere?
- Can we invent a way to do this better, cheaper, or faster?
- Can someone else do it better, cheaper, or faster than we can?

Ask radical questions and seriously consider radical answers. This is the stage we are in right now at SEMATECH. We are asking ourselves questions like these:

- What if we replace half of our journal subscriptions with a bigger investment in fax and email document delivery?
- Can we make circulation self-service?
- Can we negotiate rights to distribute some print publications electronically?
- Is it worthwhile to replace journal issues lost in circulation?
- Can we accept E-mail authorizations to charge back costs to departments?
- Can we purchase materials with a credit card instead of a detailed purchase order?
- Can we be less thorough in our cataloging?
- Can we buy fewer books and borrow from other libraries instead?
- If a given resource is not being used, should we market it or drop it?

I expect this process to result in dropping several marginal library services, assigning a few tasks to other Sematech departments or to outside contractors, and developing new ways to accomplish several remaining activities. The resulting library should closely resemble Bauwens's vision.

Find Your Power Users

Identify the power information users in your company. This task is less difficult than it may seem, because you already know these people. They are your most frequent customers, requesting lots of literature searches and SDI services, using the CD-ROM databases, and signing up for database searching classes.

Support these customers as they learn more about information tools and do whatever you can to make them successful. Make sure they are familiar with all your services and can use them effectively.

Develop a network of power users. You may be the only person who knows them all. Introduce them to one another. Hold informal seminars on information topics. Set up a database searching users' group. Ask your external information suppliers to provide specialized training sessions.

Next, put the network to work for you. Ask your power users how their teams use information. Ask them to keep information services in mind when they attend team meetings, or attend a team meeting yourself. Talk to their managers about the benefits of having an information expert in the work team.

Are questions of fact that arise in meetings answered immediately, captured to be answered later, or dropped? Does the team track technology development or industry news with an alerting service? Does the team know and use the expertise of others in the organization? Is there someone in the team who serves as an information intermediary, either by nature or by job description? Use the answers to these questions as you decide how to use your resources.

We have done this informally at Sematech for several years. Recently, we have begun a more systematic approach of identifying our power users and focusing our marketing and support on them. Our new knowledge of how Sematech functions has been invaluable as we begin setting up the network of cybrarians.

Plug In Your Cybrarians

As you map how information is gathered in your company, identify the areas that are most information-intensive and the people who are working as information intermediaries. These are the places to plug in a cybrarian.

Start with existing information intermediaries. If they aren't already power users, teach them what they need to know. Discuss training and education opportunities with them, including MLIS programs and continuing education courses. Offer your support and follow through.

Focus on management. Educate them on what librarians have to offer. Choose a key moment and show them what a professional can do to meet their information needs, either by doing it yourself or bringing in a short-term contractor. As intermediaries' positions turn over, persuade the managers to include the MLIS as a preferred qualification when advertising for a replacement. Offer to help recruit qualified candidates and bring in the very best librarians you can find.

Use your contacts to find the best potential cybrarians. Often these jobs require a unique combination of skills, possibly including specialized subject expertise, indexing, technical writing, records management, or database development, in addition to the more traditional information gathering functions of a librarian.

Once you have a cybrarian in place, collaborate with that person for success. Make sure the cybrarians are knowledgeable about the information tools available in their area. If specialized training is needed, help find out where it's available. Invite them to your staff meetings or distribute written summaries. Make sure they stay connected with you and with their counterparts throughout the company.

We are in the early stages of this process at Sematech. Two cybrarians are in place. A librarian from a member company came to Sematech for an eight-week assignment in early 1993 to work as a cybrarian in an information-intensive department. We are developing the skills of the people working as intermediaries and offering assistance to management to locate outstanding librarians to fill open positions.

Lessons for Librarians

Avoid misdefining yourself. If you define your role narrowly, as a searcher or an intermediary, you will be tempted to protect your turf and treat potential cybrarians as competition rather than colleagues. If you realize you are in the information finding, filtering, and delivery business, you can redefine your role in the company and be a leader in implementing innovative ways for your company to obtain and use information.

Encourage end-user searching. The customers who ask for passwords for on-line services are the customers you need the most. While they may or may not develop into part of your cybrarian network, you will benefit in any case.

At Sematech, we provide database searching classes on demand. The class gives us a chance to educate a receptive audience on what we do, what electronic resources exist, and how to develop an effective search strategy. While only a small portion of the people who go through search training become active searchers, they all remember that we were supportive. The goal of our end-user search training program is not to increase the number of active searchers. It is to increase the number of active library customers, and by that measure, it is effective.

Lessons for Cybrarians

Make sure your manager understands what you do. Your job is different from that of the other members of your team, and it will take a concentrated effort on your part to clearly communicate your achievements and the professional nature of your work.

Develop your knowledge of the area you work in. You do not have to have a professional degree in your area of focus, but the less education you have, the less likely you are to succeed at this challenging job. Make a concentrated effort to fill the gap. Take continuing education courses, read professional and trade journals, and rely on your professional contacts for help.

Stretch your abilities and talents to the limit. Few work teams can support a person who knows how to do only one thing. Identify and accept projects and tasks that require you to broaden your information skills. Librarians can summarize and analyze data, develop databases, negotiate with customers and suppliers, organize records for disposal or storage, or train team members in using information tools such as the Internet.

Avoid isolation. Collaborate with your corporate librarian and with your colleagues in the company to take advantage of their expertise, stay aware of new tools, and to avoid duplicate effort. Use Internet or Usenet discussion lists to keep up with both your information colleagues and your colleagues in your department's area of specialization.

A Challenge for SLA

What support can our association offer to cybrarians? While preparing this paper for presentation at SLA's Annual Conference (1993)*,   I interviewed five cybrarians. All but one were SLA members, but none was attending the conference. The reason they gave was that nothing listed in the program applied to them. What can we do to escape our library collection focus and develop programs and services applicable to this new type of special librarian?

BIBLIOGRAPHY

Bauwens, Michel. "The Emergence of the 'Cybrarian': a new organizational model for corporate libraries." *Business Information Review*, 9:4 (April 1993), pp. 65-67. (Original title as cited by Tom Peters and on PACS-L: "Cybrarians' Manifesto")

Bauwens, Michel. "Corporate Cybrary Networks: An idea whose time has come" (interview). *Internet Business Journal*, 1:1 (June-July 1993), pp. 25-27.

Chitwood, Lera. "VIPs only: Valued Information Professionals." *Competitive Intelligence Review*, Summer 1992, pp.45-46.

Peters, Tom. "Cyberpunk Librarians!" *Dallas Morning News*, April 3, 1993.

*This paper was presented at the Library Management Division Poster Session, June 8, 1993, Special Libraries Association Annual Conference.

ACKNOWLEDGMENTS

The authors gratefully acknowledge the contributions of our colleagues to this paper. Our thanks to the SEMATECH Library staff: Elisa Bass, Micheal Harper, Susanne Boatright, and Robert Wurzelbacher; the cybrarians who described their experiences: Pam Hanners and Bob Ruliffson of SEMATECH, Leslie Campbell and Lera Chitwood of Motorola, and Jennifer Armstrong of National Semiconductor; Bob Guz, Susan Rogers, Mary Holland, and Michel Bauwens; and the contributors to the VISIONS and LIBADMIN Internet discussion lists.

Nancy Elder
Head, Life Science Library
The General Libraries
The University of Texas at Austin
LLNIE@utxdp.dp.utexas.edu

15. REACH OUT ELECTRONICALLY: DELIVERING SERVICE OUTSIDE THE LIBRARY

While librarians stereotypically sit and wait for users to arrive in the library, this is not a realistic or productive expectation for the special library. Outreach is one of our most valuable marketing tools. It is essential to extend a hand to current and potential users, actively recruiting them as clientele and furthering the corporate goal of profit making by providing service to them. Outreach serves several purposes:

- delivering information directly to customers
- marketing
- raising the visibility of the information center
- establishing the information center as relevant, knowledgeable, interested, and involved
- hooking users into more use

Libraries can provide outreach services in many ways. Newsletters, current awareness services, and selective dissemination of information are typical outreach services. These three are well documented in the literature, but in the past were time-consuming to produce. With the recent growth of electronic formats, wider availability of microcomputers, and attendant ease of use, it is wise to consider, or reconsider, the application of these services in small special libraries.

It is somewhat daunting to read about the monumental services offered by special library giants such as AT&T. These services can easily be scaled to the staff, equipment, and budget available. The focus here will be on the kinds of outreach services that a one-person or small special library may reasonably offer by using electronic resources.

As you consider implementing outreach services be sure to keep your own schedule, library staff, hardware availability, and other commitments in mind. The newsletter or current awareness bulletin that is new and fun for a few issues may not seem so fun after a few months. As you contemplate a new service make sure that you can keep up with it. It is counterproductive and damaging to user confidence to start a service, have your users love it, and then not be able to keep up with it. Design a service that is:

- easy to produce
- of manageable length
- of manageable frequency
- good enough to replace an existing service or task should the choice be necessary

SDI and Current Awareness Services

Selective dissemination of information (SDI) and current awareness services are closely related but differ in the intent to deliver more, or less, customized service. SDI is a long, elaborate name for a sensible and not very difficult idea. SDI is sending to individual users information that is relevant to their particular interest. Simply put, send only the "good stuff," rather than a newsletter or comprehensive list of sources that the user will then have to dig through. Current awareness services encompass the idea of SDI, but the term may also refer specifically to a service that involves scanning a larger body of literature to "stay current" rather than focusing as narrowly as is typically found in SDI.

Both of these services lend themselves to electronic delivery. Options for electronic production and delivery range from the very high tech to requiring only a modest setup likely to be found in most companies. The librarian can choose from a number of options to deliver services electronically: set up individual profiles through commercial vendors, use a locally mounted database (e.g., CD-ROM) to run individualized profiles on a regular basis, set up broader profiles for project teams or departments rather than for individuals. Each of these options has different features and costs.

SDI USING COMMERCIAL VENDORS

The choice of vendors offering SDI services seems almost infinite. You will want to consider features such as timing, cost, format, and appropriateness of databases. These services that offer E-mail or ftp delivery give you the option of having them delivered directly to your user and, perhaps, reuse of the data in digital format. Evaluate the features of directly competing services for your users.

- How easily can the file be manipulated for printing or loading into a reference manager?
- Does your company already provide accounts for staff on the service used or will you have to set up and manage a large number of special accounts?
- Will one vendor cover the needs of many of your users or will you have to set up and maintain accounts with several vendors?

The costs of these services can be considerable. If you set up service through commercial vendors, explore thoroughly, in advance, what the projected costs will be. Will costs be assigned to the library or to individuals and projects? Can you afford to offer the service to all interested staff or will you need to "qualify" those desiring service?

SDI ON A LOCALLY MOUNTED DATABASE

A viable option may be to purchase the most relevant database or databases on CD-ROM and run individual profiles each time you receive an updated disk for the database. With a modest investment of time and PC know-how, you can probably develop a script or batch file that will automatically execute your profiles. This approach allows you to provide similar service at an established price, paid annually. If you have many users, the direct costs could be substantially less than having the SDIs provided through a vendor. This approach also has the advantage of providing you with a database for retrospective searching (see Electronic Reference section) and the option to network the CD-ROM. However, there are tradeoffs in labor and timeliness. Setting aside time to run and print the SDIs is a labor cost to the library. In addition, most of the CD-ROM databases run several weeks to several months behind the updates available on-line.

CURRENT AWARENESS SERVICES

As a variation on a theme, current awareness services serve many of the same functions and can be provided in some of the same ways as SDI. There are other more specialized current awareness services that are available in electronic format or lend themselves to electronic delivery. Commercial current awareness services, such as journal routing, title page routing, and article routing, are outreach services worth exploring. They are more appealing now that you have electronic options for delivery.

Journal routing and article routing by attaching a routing slip and letting the item wend its way through a list of potentially interested users are easy and relatively ineffective. Timeliness is lost and, not infrequently, so is the item. These two techniques do not lend themselves to electronic delivery unless you are prepared to deal with complicated copyright issues. Commercial print services such as Current Contents or CAS Alerts (from Chemical Abstracts) are possible alternatives. They carry the disadvantages of journal routing as issues are delayed on a vacationing user's desk or lost in the shuffle.

Current Contents on Disk (with or without abstracts) affords the possibility of electronic delivery. Weekly issues arrive on floppy disk to be loaded on a microcomputer. Users could use them directly in the library with stored profiles. You might execute stored profiles for your users and then send the printed results. Or, best yet, you might execute stored profiles and send the file on the company E-mail or network directly to the user's workstation. If there is a suitable network in place, consider paying the extra cost for a site license so that the service is available directly to the user. For the additional cost of the license, you can provide the service without having to manage the profiles.

Newsletters and Library Bulletins

Regular newsletters or occasional library bulletins can be an effective method of reminding users of regular services and materials, of informing them about new services, or alerting them to special events. However, producing, printing, and distributing the newsletter is time consuming. Review the electronic resources available and see if you can accomplish the same result with less work. You company LAN, server, or E-mail system lets you deliver your newsletter quickly and directly to only those who are interested. If the E-mail option is available, you should be able to develop a "subscription" list, prepare the newsletter in the E-mail system, and then, with one keystroke, deliver that issue simultaneously to all subscribers. If you do not have E-mail, you may be able to have a folder or file on a server. You can post the newsletter whenever you want, and your users can access and open the document to see your information center news.

X. A CASE STUDY

We can talk about the library without walls, we can dream about it, we can plan for it, but what is it like to work in one? What are its strengths and weaknesses? The next article is a case study written by a librarian who works in a totally electronic library--one with no journals, books, technical reports, standards, or patents.. That's right--none. Beth Dupuis works in a library service center--a sort of information catalog store--a place where you order up what you want and it is delivered to you.

Beth Dupuis
Balcones Library Service Center
The General Libraries
The University of Texas at Austin
LLBAD@utxdp.dp.utexas.edu

16. THE ALL-ELECTRONIC BALCONES LIBRARY SERVICE CENTER

Electronic libraries are often labeled "libraries without walls" because they rely on their connection to other libraries, information centers, and sources of data that are not physically within the library itself. Looking at the Balcones Library Service Center, you may think that it is more correctly described as a library that has only walls--and a few computer terminals.

The Balcones Library Service Center is a blending of academic and special libraries. Although administered through the General Libraries of The University of Texas at Austin, it caters to university employees who work at the Balcones Research Center (BRC), a science and technology research center located about fifteen miles from the main campus. The BRC community is a mixture of 15 agencies, composed of 1,500 researchers, staff, and students, whose concentrations include geology, archaeology, paleontology, water resources, energy, nuclear engineering, materials science, microelectronics, electromechanics, and high-performance computing. We function as an information convenience store, trying to supply the largest quantity of goods to the largest number of customers in the fastest manner possible. The main difference is that, instead of a twenty-four-hour-a-day operation, our doors are open only four hours a day during the work week.

Mission

As any library, our goal is to provide the best, most efficient service to our community. Many of our first-time users look confused when they don't see many books or journals stored on our shelves. Some conclude that the library "doesn't have anything" for them. Unfortunately, it takes quite a bit of marketing and promotion to convince them that although this facility doesn't collect the "stuff" that they are used to seeing, it nonetheless makes many useful resources available to them. Our mission is to provide these researchers and students with the same type of information they could receive on campus. The format may be electronic rather than print, or it may take a few extra days to retrieve an item from campus via courier, but we strive for efficiency and accuracy. Not surprisingly, we are concerned only with accessing and delivering information, not with preserving it.

Services

One of our most heavily used services is the courier service of retrieving books and materials from the campus. We check out books and other sources for patrons whenever possible and also copy items that are in magazines and journals too new to be loaned. Copying services are on a cost-recovery basis. The courier service is dependent upon quick and reliable communication between the library assistant in the service center and the runner. A patron may request a book in person by filling out a request form, or may send an E-mail message to the library assistant. Once the information has been verified, it is sent either by E-mail or fax to the courier on campus for retrieval. The university provides a system-wide mail service for shuttling materials back and forth.

Verification is probably one of the most time-consuming activities and occasionally one of the most challenging, especially for conference proceedings. This may require us to turn to sources such as RLIN, OCLC, or Dialog. In many cases, this will also lead us to request the item from the interlibrary loan office.

Additionally, we handle reference questions. Often this leads us to searching on-line sources and occasionally will require us to call another library with a print source. Most of the time our reference tools, such as *Books in Print, Ulrich's, Encyclopedia of Associations,* and *Who's Who,* will be enough. As I will discuss later, we also perform many electronic services and spend time assisting patrons in choosing the correct sources to search on their own. Perhaps one of the most time-consuming aspects is teaching patrons which sources are most appropriate for their needs and giving them value-added assistance in evaluating the information retrieved.

Resources

STAFF

The Balcones Library is staffed by two employees: one librarian, one library assistant, and two runners, for a total of two full-time employees. The librarian is mainly responsible for performing on-line searches on OCLC, RLIN, Dialog, and Lexis/Nexis, devising informational handouts and newsletters, developing new services, and attending campus meetings. The library assistant is the head of circulation services, responsible for charges, renewals, requests, bills, and statistics. He also performs many on-line searches, assists patrons with searching, works closely with the runners, orders supplies, and processes all interlibrary loan requests. Based at the Engineering Library on the main campus, the runners organize the daily fax and E-mail requests, retrieve the books and copies from the appropriate libraries, and send them out to us. One day a week a runner works at BRC to maintain close contact with the library assistant and our patrons.

PRINT TOOLS

Our print collection includes leisure reading magazines, newspapers, older editions of basic reference sources, donated paperbacks, and some related indexes. With the variety of research interests at this center, it would be financially impossible to subscribe to even one critical journal in each field. The only option available to the Balcones Library, as a remote site of the main library system, is to rely on electronic information and a circulation system similar to document delivery.

ELECTRONIC TOOLS

Appropriately enough for an electronic library, our most useful tools are the UTCAT Plus on-line catalog, our staff search stations, and the LAN workstation. As with any library, the catalog assists users in selecting titles and staff in confirming location, call number, and availability of items. On the UTCAT Plus terminals, three general periodical indexes are also available that assist some patrons with finding general references.

Staff have workstations, which provide our access to electronic information. Often we utilize the bibliographic databases, such as RLIN and OCLC, when locating items not owned by The University of Texas and when verifying conference proceedings. These same terminals allow us access to the hundreds of electronic, mainly bibliographic, databases from Dialog. We do many ready reference searches, and some full-service searches, and we allow patrons to schedule and perform U-SEARCHes. Each service varies slightly from the rest. The ready reference searches are used when we think that this is a concise, quick-answer question that any library would be able to provide with its print or electronic sources; these costs are covered by the library system.

Full-service searching is offered to patrons who want a more complex set of queries answered or want to cover a wider time frame. In many cases, a researcher will request full-service search to locate all the relevant literature published on his or her narrow field of interest before embarking on a new project. The searching will be performed by the librarian or library assistant, but the patron will be charged for the total cost incurred. Either of these two services can be filled using any of the databases available through the vendors.

The third service, U-SEARCH, is offered at Balcones as well as some other libraries on the main campus. This option is a compromise of the two already discussed. Offered by Dialog as an instructional system called Knowledge Index, U-SEARCH provides select databases for the patrons themselves to search for a set time and cost regardless of the number of databases searched. I call this a compromise because the patrons have the longer amount of time and the cheaper cost combined, but also have fewer resources to choose from and must rely on their own searching skills.

One of the newest options for our patrons is the introduction of a terminal that links our library with a CD-ROM LAN at the main library on campus. Although this system is in its "terrible twos" stage, we are learning a lot about the ups and downs of a local area network. Occasionally, the system will already have the allotted number of users searching or our connection will be cut, but it seems that the "ups" are well worth it. Since the system is relatively new, people in the different fields of study are waiting to have relevant indexes mounted on the LAN. Once again, since our community has such specialized interests, no single source will please everyone; but many people search the *Applied Science and Technology Index* and *MEDLINE*. Also, the addition of *Dissertation Abstracts* and *Science Citation Index* has increased the scope of our resources and has sparked new interest in our services. The benefits of this system are that all searching is free to university staff and students and that many users can access the same database from different locations. In our case, the LAN is our current and future link to the databases on campus; once they are mounted, our staff has the same ability to search them as do patrons at other libraries on campus.

FUTURE DEVELOPMENTS

Paying close attention to our users' information needs and habits, as well as the new technologies and options that may be of assistance to them, is one of our primary concerns. Mastery of new technology, and an understanding of the benefits and drawbacks of that technology, may be the leverage you need to maintain your library's status in times of restricted funding. It is difficult in any library setting to keep up with the latest trends in all the relevant areas of interest, but a visible effort can make a world of difference to regular and soon-to-be-regular users.

When I first started in the position of Balcones Librarian, I conducted a brief survey of the employees at BRC to determine their fields of study, current use of libraries, and suggestions for our future development. The two types of comments that I remember most were "Thanks for showing such enthusiasm. Keep it up!" and "I didn't even know what it was before." Although library users and nonusers probably don't want to be incessantly bombarded with library surveys and information, it is important to find out what services they think should be there and what they would use if it were available. Recently I started a monthly one-page newsletter to publicize new CD-ROM products on the LAN, improvements in our courier service, and announcements of workshops on information sources and searching. Through their comments, I have learned that many researchers now feel that they know what the library does and how that benefits them. If the library is investing in new technologies, shouldn't the users know about it?

The University of Texas has committed itself to participating in the evolution of the electronic environment. The development of the LAN was the first step; our next step was the installation of terminals that give the university community easy access to the Internet. I don't expect the Internet will be a highly utilized resource in our library. First, items available have variable lifespans; some resources disappear without notice. Second, there is no standardization to the search methods for the items that you can access. Each new database and OPAC is a new package to learn. Third, many of the patrons interested have already investigated by connecting through their personal computers. I don't think that we will have too many people interested in spending the time to wade through the murky waters of the Internet. On the other hand, those who have already taken the dive into the "net" will probably be asking us questions that will test the limits of our knowledge.

Summary

What is it really truly like? To be truthful, sometimes it is very odd to look around the library and see very few books and almost no shelving. This is even more disconcerting to some potential users, who ignored us at first because we didn't look like a library. But what is probably the oddest fact is that I can't participate in collection development. When academic librarians get together, especially science and technology librarians, a major topic of discussion and gossip is the high cost of journals and who's going to collect materials in a new area. They can discuss a topic like "nanotechnology" for a goodly amount of time. While I can act as a moderator or "the voice or reason," I can't really participate in discussions of what books and journals to buy or what journals to cancel. While this is going to change in the future, these activities are a very big part of what most librarians do today.

Another problem is that, because we are so unlike other libraries, many of my colleagues forget that our users must be treated differently from people on campus. Our users can't just "come by" and browse — items that are marked for "library use only" create problems for our users. We often need to remind our colleagues that exceptions must be made willingly and gracefully.

But the advantages outweigh the problems. I am in a position to experience directly what it means to be "an electronic librarian." And I can serve as a model for other UT librarians--especially those who may be a bit uneasy about the direction of library service. I can demonstrate that service is service and reference is reference regardless of whether we do it with books or with networks.

CONCLUSION--WHAT DOES IT ALL MEAN?

The electronic library is about progress, but progress is meaningless if we don't know where we're going. So, just where are we headed? Are we headed for oblivion, information nirvana, or something in between? All of us who participated in this book believe that we are headed toward something in between. We will have easier access to more information that is less controlled by indexes, library catalogs, and publishers, but at the same time, people will continue to want access to books and periodicals that they do not want to buy. This trend is demonstrated by a recent Consumer Research study. CR found that 65% of all U.S. households bought at least one book and 822 million adult books were sold between April 1991 and March 1992. This is a lot of book purchases, and in the same period public library circulation was up 15%. To us this means that new technologies do not drive out old; rather new technologies work to increase and sustain each other.

Easier access to information has definitely increased on-site usage, interlibrary loan, and document delivery. We have discovered that electronic access indexes bring more requests for new journals, books, and conference proceedings, rather than fewer. We regularly get requests from new users. Networked access and E-mail citations from colleagues mean that people who never before "darkened our doors" now request copies.

Delivering information to homes, offices, and cars is only part of what will be needed. Users (information consumers) will need ways to navigate the various systems and access tools. Cable TV is a good example, as more and more TV channels are added, it will no longer be possible for users to "channel surf"--to run quickly through the channels or switch between already known likely candidates (say PBS, A&E, TLC, and etc.). How will users find what they want to watch when there are 200, 500, or 1,000 TV channels? Even today those of us with cable throw away--don't watch--most of what comes to us on the cable. What libraries and individuals will need is a customized subset.

Many decisions will be made over the next few years, the first being who will pay for these services: individuals, taxpayers, or a combination of both. We already know people will use whatever taxpayers will support, but how much will they want to pay for electronic access to articles delivered right to their computer or TV? Some believe that individuals will pay $40 to $50 a month. But many think less, including Wendy Sanko, director of business development for US West Communications. She believes that most individuals will pay only "significantly less than the cost a large pizza." August Grant, a professor of communications at the University of Texas at Austin, believes that "there's a ceiling on the percentage of real income most people will spend" on information.   This ceiling already exists for libraries-- corporate or other.

We have just begun to plan our travels down the electronic information highway. The road will be both evolutionary and revolutionary, and it will take some time. And we will all need this time to think about:

- choosing the right technology
- getting the knowledge to make specific technologies work
- figuring out security, access, and maintenance procedures
- getting a plan and then revising it regularly
- marketing the product and its capabilities
- upgrading our information

If we think about all these things carefully, and then act appropriately on our conclusions, we should be ready for the future. The risks of not investing or participating are increasing. Lack of innovation, conservatism, and timidity can have devastating results. Without risk, no growth or change is possible. Our book is the beginning of our exploration; we hope it is the beginning of your explorations too.